YESTERDAY'S BREAD

YESTERDAY'S BREAD

100 Creative Recipes for Not-Quite-Fresh Bread

CAROLE LALLI

HarperPerennial

A Division of HarperCollinsPublishers

FIRST EDITION

Designed by Joel Avirom and Jason Snyder

Lalli, Carole, 1942–
    Yesterday's bread:one hundred creative recipes for not-quite-fresh bread /Carole Lalli.—1st ed.
       p.   cm.
     ISBN: 0-06-095314-4
     1. Cookery (Bread)   I. Title.
   TX769.L26   1999
   641.8'15—dc21   99-26365

---

99 00 01 02 03 ❖/RRD 10 9 8 7 6 5 4 3 2 1

To the bakers.
And to the generations
of clever home cooks
who taught us that yesterday's
bread is today's treasure.

CONT

E N T S

ACKNOWLEDGMENTS

A few years ago, Jennifer Griffin was an editorial assistant with a very good idea, a book of recipes for dishes based on stale bread. It wasn't Jennifer's last good idea, and today she is a senior editor. Thanks, Jennifer.

Ellen Morrissey picked up the thread during the editing process and was cheerful and efficient to the end.

One morning I told my editor—and dear friend—Susan Friedland that I had made a pudding with pumpkin puree and pumpernickel bread that was no longer suitable for the table, and she said, "That doesn't sound so good." Otherwise, she has been ever enthusiastic, helpful, and supportive. (Susan was wrong for once; the recipe for Pumpkin-Pumpernickel Bread Pudding can be found on page 128.)

Frank, Nina, Carla, and Fernando were good tasters and good sports. One evening, Nina defined the process of developing and testing recipes: "What's for dinner? Let me guess. Something with bread in, under, or over it?"

INTRODUCTION

If wasting food is a sin, it seems that wasting bread is even more so. For centuries bread was, in Western cultures, what rice was in the East—the centerpiece of meals and often the most nutritious dish. The importance of bread in people's lives cannot be overstated. Bread was sacred. From Exodus in the Old Testament to Christ's teachings in the New, the references are numerous.

Whether sacred or profane, recycling stale bread into other dishes was a necessity for people who could not afford to waste a scrap, and out of that necessity some wonderful dishes were born. Pain perdu may mean lost bread but it really is found again in French toast, one of the stars of the recycled bread repertoire, not to mention the Sunday brunch menu. Stuffings transform the ordinary into the special—the Thanksgiving turkey is perhaps the single most ceremonial dish in our culture, but it wouldn't have half its significance unstuffed. The stuffing, of course, is almost invariably made of bread, garnished to one degree or another. The earliest bread soup may be Roman. It doesn't sound like much of a treat—stale bread mashed up with water—but from those beginnings rose so many bread-based soups that they easily form a subcategory of their own: Gazpacho and Pappa al Pomodoro are merely two examples. And, while English summer pudding comes from an impulse to use up a glut of berries and yesterday's bread, it also is a celebration of ingredients and a fairly perfect dessert.

This book grew out of the very old compulsion to be prudent, and, I think, respectful, regarding bread. But it could not have occurred without the rebirth of bread that is one of today's strongest contemporary food trends. My mother's generation came up with the phrase "the greatest thing since sliced bread," but mine seems hell-bent on restoring artisanal baking and bringing "honest loaves" to every chic urban neighborhood. Farmer's markets, specialty stores, and, yes, supermarkets, are sources for sturdy handmade loaves; Americans who want good bread can get it wherever they get the rest of their groceries.

At the same time that we are finding good bread in our markets, we seem to be nearly obsessed with baking it at home. In the last decade, the bread machine has become one of the most popular new home cooking appliances, and bread books by a new generation of professional bakers have proliferated.

It is the very nature of these breads—often fat- and certainly preservative-free—that almost demands that we have second lives in mind for them. They lose freshness quickly, even if they do not go quite stale in a day. It is the nature of a French baguette that requires at least one trip a day to the neighborhood boulangerie—and inventiveness on the part of the frugal home cook.

This book is built on the tradition of turning good bread into worthy dishes that would not be met with any sense of deprivation from those served. By now, these are first-class dishes for which no apologies are necessary. My best hope for those who use this book is that they first find useful ways of making fine dishes from otherwise good bread that has lost its first luster. Beyond that, I hope they find themselves planning ahead, as I do, to secure the right bread for a favorite bread pudding or bread salad or stuffing that just wouldn't be right made with fresh bread.

Yesterday's Bread Basics

Not far from where I live is one of New York's finest food markets, which also is one of the city's largest and best bakers. In the bread department, surrounding the fragrant breads of the day is an impressive display of packaged bread products, all carrying the shop's label. Thin crisps from every sort of bread made there, along with plain and flavored croutons, stuffings, and crumbs line the shelves. The message was obvious: Yesterday's bread is today's pantry treasure. But there's no need to pay for such items if you have a surfeit of your own homemade or store-bought bread. Here are some methods for recycling not-so-fresh-bread into croutons and crumbs. For preparing Crisps, see page 23.

CROUTONS

Your own croutons, cheaper and so much better than any that come in packages, are best stored in paper bags in the pantry or, for longer periods, frozen in plastic containers or bags. Use croutons on salads or soups or serve them with drinks. Croutons also can be used for stuffings or ground to crumbs and used to coat foods before frying or baking.

The combinations of seasonings given here are merely suggestions, and I encourage you to develop your own, especially when you have a particular dish in mind and are looking for compatible flavors in the croutons that will garnish it.

The methods that follow are based on 8 slices of day-old bread cut into 1-inch cubes. If you have more or fewer slices, the quantities of seasonings can be adjusted accordingly.

METHOD 1: Preheat the oven to 400°. Spread the cubes on a baking sheet and place in the oven. Stir the croutons up from time to time until they are fairly uniformly toasted on all sides.

Place 1 tablespoon of olive oil in a large mixing bowl and add any of the combinations of herbs and spices that follow. Toss the cubes well with the seasonings.

METHOD 2: Place ¼ cup olive oil in a large skillet over moderate heat. Add the bread cubes and cook, turning them over every minute or so, until they are crisp and golden brown all over, 5–10 minutes. Lower the heat if necessary to avoid burning the cubes or cooking them unevenly, and do not rush the process. Sprinkle any of the combinations of herbs and spices and salt to taste over the cubes and cook a minute or so longer. Drain the croutons on paper towels.

TEX-MEX

1 teaspoon ground chili powder

½ teaspoon cumin

1 teaspoon dried oregano

½ cup mixed fresh herbs

½ cup kosher or sea salt

SWEET SPICES

1 teaspoon ground ginger

1 teaspoon ground cinnamon

1 teaspoon ground cloves

½ teaspoon ground nutmeg

½ teaspoon ground cardamom

MEDITERRANEAN

*2 cloves garlic, minced and sautéed
   to a light golden brown*

*4 tablespoons mixed fresh herbs
   (rosemary, thyme, marjoram,
   parsley), minced*

INDIAN

1 teaspoon curry powder

1 teaspoon ground ginger

*1 teaspoon freshly ground
   white pepper*

2 teaspoons turmeric

CRUMBS

Like croutons, homemade crumbs are better than store-bought. Crumbs can easily be produced in a food processor and stored for a week or so in paper or plastic bags in the refrigerator or for longer in the freezer. You can combine different stale breads to produce a blended crumb mix or keep crumbs from different breads separately and use them for different dishes (light breads for coating fish or chicken; whole grains for vegetable stuffings, and so on).

Alternatively, you can keep a chunk of stale bread in your bread box or basket and grate it as needed.

STUFFING

With few exceptions, I prefer large crumbs or cubes, rather than finely ground bread crumbs, for stuffings. Fine crumbs tend to produce a tight, dense texture, sometimes unpleasantly moist. They are fine, however, used as a topping for mushrooms or clams or to coat food before sautéing, broiling, or frying.

See pages 71–73 for recipes for stuffing poultry and pages 98–99 for vegetable stuffings.

BRUSCHETTE, CROUTONS, CROSTINI, SANDWICHES, AND CRISPS

Crostini and canapés are small pieces of bread topped with a puree or pâté, or a piece of cured meat or cheese. They are served with drinks or as part of an antipasto, with a plate of salami and prosciutto, or with grilled or stuffed vegetables. Toasted croutons and crostini can be served with soup or salad.

A bruschetta is a piece of bread that has been grilled—preferably—or toasted and in its simplest form is brushed with oil, or first rubbed with the exposed side of a garlic clove that has been cut in half and then brushed with oil; it is one of the best things you can eat. In Tuscany a slice of grilled and oiled bread is called fettunta, and often is served in place of bread or along with other breads at the start of a meal. The toppings for croutons, crostini, and bruschette are somewhat interchangeable, but, generally speaking, a bruschetta is larger, thicker, and more substantial than a crouton.

A bruschetta sometimes is fried. Olive oil is heated in a skillet, a piece or two of garlic is browned in it, and finally the bread is cooked to a golden brown on both sides. Bread cooked in this manner can be served alone, as part of an antipasto, or with soup or salad; or, it can be cut into cubes and served, like croutons, *on* soup or salad.

CATALAN TOMATO BREAD

———

NINA'S TOMATO BRUSCHETTA

———

PAN BAGNAT

———

BRUSCHETTA WITH
PUREED SALT COD

———

MUSHROOM RAGU
FOR BRUSCHETTA

———

SPICY CLAMS BRUSCHETTA

———

BRUSCHETTA WITH
WHITE BEAN PUREE

———

CROSTINI OR CROUTONS
WITH ANCHOVIES AND BUTTER

———

ROASTED RED PEPPER SPREAD
FOR CROUTONS OR CROSTINI

———

SHRIMP TOAST

TUSCAN CHICKEN
LIVER CROSTINI

———

TOMATO CROSTINI

———

CHEDDAR-SAGE TOAST

———

MOZZARELLA IN CARROZZA

———

TOASTED CAPRESE SANDWICHES

———

CRISPS

———

SPREADS AND DIPS

Pesto

Aioli

Anchovy Sauce

Salsa

Tapenade

Tuna Tapenade

Olive Spreads

Cream Cheese Spreads

Flavored Butters

CATALAN TOMATO BREAD

8 servings

In its most minimal, and possibly best-loved version, the toasted bread is simply rubbed with the cut side of a tomato; with no other ingredients to hide behind, only the best high-summer ripe tomato will do. With a salad, a slice or two of tomato bread can make for an incredibly satisfying lunch; it also is a great starter for a summer dinner.

1 day-old French baguette or 8 slices day-old country-type bread

2 large ripe tomatoes (about 1½ pounds)

Cut the bread on the diagonal into slices barely ½ inch thick; toast or grill the slices lightly. Cut the tomatoes in half horizontally, then rub the cut sides over the toast on both sides, squeezing very gently if necessary to release the juice but not the pulp.

If made ahead, the bread can be briefly retoasted.

VARIATIONS:

Place 2 lightly smashed cloves of peeled garlic into a ¼ cup extra-virgin olive oil and let sit for about 10 minutes. Brush the toast with the oil before rubbing with the tomato.

For a more substantial dish the tomato bread can be layered with thin slices of Spanish Serrano ham or prosciutto and/or Parmigiano Reggiano or Manchego cheese.

NINA'S TOMATO BRUSCHETTA

4–8 servings

In high summer, the perfume of my daughter's own version of this classic drifts ahead of the platter she carries toward us, most often on a sunny Sunday afternoon when "a little something" is called for between brunch and late dinner. These are most sublime on grilled bread, so if you are firing up for another dish, you might want to plan them for a first course, or as part of an antipasto.

4 medium ripe tomatoes

½ teaspoon sea salt

4 large or 8 small slices Tuscan, country, or other sturdy bread

3 cloves garlic, peeled

¼ cup extra-virgin olive oil

8–10 fresh basil leaves, torn into shreds

Chop the tomatoes and sprinkle with the salt; set aside for about 15 minutes.

Meanwhile, grill or toast the bread. Cut one of the garlic cloves in half and rub it over the warm bread, then lightly brush the bread with some of the oil.

Chop the remaining garlic. Place the remaining oil in a small skillet over medium heat; add the garlic and cook, stirring, until it is just golden. Cool the oil and garlic slightly, then stir it into the tomatoes. Distribute the tomato mixture over the bread, top with the basil, and serve at once.

VARIATIONS:

Dice about 4 ounces of mozzarella and add it to the tomato mixture.

Shave ricotta salata cheese over the tomatoes.

Omit the oil and garlic and spread the bread with Pesto (page 24), then top with the chopped tomatoes.

PAN BAGNAT

4–8 servings

Essentially a sandwich version of salade Niçoise, **Pan Bagnat** can be made on French bread, slices of country-style white or whole-wheat bread, or on a sturdy roll. As an open-faced sandwich, Pan Bagnat can be served as a first course, bridging the categories of salad and bruschetta; on small rounds of French baguette, they can be part of a selection of canapés to serve with aperitifs.

8 slices country-style white or whole-wheat bread

1 clove garlic, peeled

4 tablespoons olive oil

1 tablespoon red wine vinegar

Coarse salt

Freshly ground pepper

1 small red onion, sliced

4 medium tomatoes, sliced

1 bunch radishes, washed, trimmed, and sliced

1 can (6½- or 7-ounce) tuna, imported French or Italian if possible

4 anchovy fillets, washed and drained if salted, drained if packed in oil, chopped

Fresh parsley or basil leaves

Toast or grill the bread and lay the slices out on a work surface or cutting board. Cut the garlic in half and rub it over one side of the bread slices; brush the bread with the olive oil, sprinkle the vinegar over, and season to taste with salt and pepper. Divide the remaining ingredients among four of the slices of bread and cover with the remaining slices. Place heavy plates on the sandwiches for about 5 minutes, then serve.

NOTE: The filling ingredients can be roughly chopped together for an open-faced sandwich or bruschetta or more finely chopped and mounded on toasted bread rounds for canapés.

BRUSCHETTA WITH PUREED SALT COD

6–8 servings

This is one of my favorite snacks. One salt cod bruschetta and one of tomato make an easy first course in a casual dinner with pasta or hearty soup as the entree. The pieces also can be cut into small squares to serve with drinks.

½ pound prepared salt cod (see Note)

2 cloves garlic, peeled

Freshly ground white or black pepper

⅓–½ cup extra-virgin olive oil

6–12 slices day-old country-style bread or baguette

Italian parsley leaves (about ¼ cup), chopped

Sea salt or kosher salt (optional)

Break the fish up into pieces and place them in the bowl of a food processor. Pulse two or three times. Add one of the garlic cloves, a generous amount of pepper, and a bit of the olive oil; continue to process, slowly adding the oil, to form a rough puree.

Lightly toast or grill the bread. Cut the remaining garlic clove in half and rub the cut sides over the bread. Spread the puree over the slices, drizzle with a bit more of the oil, and sprinkle the parsley over. It is unlikely that salt will be needed, but if it is, the sea salt can be passed at the table.

NOTE: Excellent quality presoaked salt cod is now widely available, even in supermarkets. The fish needs to be soaked again—in a large basin or bowl of cool water—overnight or at least for 10 or 12 hours, with a few changes of water. Remove the fish from the water and place it on paper towels to eliminate all excess water. Examine the fish for bones and remove any that you find (more than a couple, if any, is unlikely).

Salt cod is a modestly priced item, so it is worth paying extra for the best one your fishmonger recommends as it will be easiest to prepare and will have least waste.

Mushroom Ragu for Bruschetta

4 servings

1 ounce dried porcini or other wild
   mushrooms

1 shallot, peeled

1 clove garlic, peeled

½ pound cremini, shiitake, portobello, or other wild variety mushrooms, or mixed wild, or wild
   and white cultivated mushrooms

1 tablespoon butter

1 tablespoon olive oil

3 large sage leaves, minced

½ cup Italian parsley leaves,
   minced

2 tablespoons crème fraîche or
   heavy cream

Salt

Freshly ground pepper

4–6 slices Tuscan-type bread,
   ½ inch thick

White truffle–flavored olive oil
   (optional)

Place the dried mushrooms in a small bowl and add water to cover; let the mushrooms steep for 20 minutes. Drain the dried mushrooms, reserving the soaking liquid, then place them in paper towels to absorb the excess moisture.

Mince the shallot and garlic. Trim the stem end of the fresh mushrooms, wipe away any soil, and slice the caps. Place the butter and oil in a medium skillet over medium-high heat. When the butter ceases foaming, add the shallot and garlic; cook, stirring, for a few minutes, until they are softened but not browned. Mince the reconstituted dried mushrooms, add them to the skillet, and cook for a minute.

Add the sliced caps to the skillet, turn the heat up slightly, and cook, stirring, until the mushrooms are wilted; do not overcook them. Measure out ¼ cup of the reserved mushroom water and add it to the skillet; cook, stirring, until most of the liquid evaporates. Stir in the sage, half the parsley, and the crème fraîche and cook for about 30 seconds longer. Season to taste with salt and pepper.

Grill or toast the bread on both sides. Divide the mushroom mixture among the slices, drizzle each with a bit of truffle oil, and sprinkle the additional parsley over.

SPICY CLAMS BRUSCHETTA

6 servings

Whenever my family is in Italy we manage to spend a day at Fregene, a beach town outside Rome. The main attraction is Da Mastino, a family-run restaurant with the two features one craves and rarely finds in seaside eateries: breathtaking excellence and an unimaginably relaxed atmosphere.

6 ounces tiny clams in jar
(see Note)

3 tablespoons olive oil plus
additional for the bread

3 cloves garlic, peeled and
minced

Big pinch (or more) crushed
hot red pepper flakes

¾ cup chopped tomato

3 tablespoons chopped parsley

Sea salt or kosher salt

Freshly ground pepper

6 large slices Tuscan-type or
other country bread, white
or part whole-wheat

This dish approximates a favorite from Da Mastino. Unfortunately, the fresh tiny clams the Italians call *vongole veraci* (true clams) are not available here, but you can find good-quality imported ones in jars at specialty food markets.

Drain the clams, rinse with cold water, and drain well.

Pour the 3 tablespoons oil into a medium-size skillet over moderate heat. Add the garlic and hot pepper and cook, stirring, until the garlic is golden but not darkened. Add the clams and cook for about 30 seconds. Add the tomato, raise the heat, and cook, stirring, for about another minute to let some of the moisture burn off. Remove the pan from the heat and stir in the parsley and salt and pepper to taste.

Grill or toast the bread on both sides. Brush the bread lightly with oil and divide the clam mixture among the slices.

NOTE: The number of jars of clams you will need will depend on their size. The ones I use come in 2-ounce jars.

Bruschetta with White Bean Puree

8 servings

Drain the beans and place them in a pot. Add the broth and enough water, if necessary, to cover by about 1½ inches. Smash and peel 2 of the garlic cloves and add them to the pot along with the sage or rosemary and a generous grinding of pepper. Bring to a low boil over medium heat, then lower the heat and cook until the beans are soft, 30–40 minutes.

½ pound cannellini beans, soaked overnight

2 cups chicken broth

3 cloves garlic

1 large or 2 small sprigs fresh sage or 1 sprig fresh rosemary

Freshly ground black pepper

2 tablespoons olive oil plus additional for the bread

8 slices country-type bread, each about 1 inch thick

Minced parsley

Drain the beans, reserving the cooking liquid. Discard the sage or rosemary but not the garlic. Return the cooking liquid to the saucepan, place over medium heat, and bring to a simmer; cook until the liquid is reduced to about 1 cup.

Place the beans, the 2 tablespoons of olive oil, and a bit of the reduced liquid into the bowl of a food processor. Use the pulse button or turn the machine on and off to produce a rough puree, adding additional liquid as needed.

Grill or toast the bread. Cut the remaining garlic clove in half and rub it over one side of the bread slices; brush the slices lightly with olive oil and spread a thick layer of the bean puree over. Drizzle a tiny bit more of the oil over each portion and sprinkle with the parsley.

CROSTINI OR CROUTONS
WITH ANCHOVIES AND BUTTER

6 servings

When I was little, these were an adored treat I often shared with my grandfather. This and his bread salad are the only dishes I can remember him preparing—perhaps recycling bread was his secret passion. I still find bread, butter, and anchovies—mindlessly simple—a sublime treat.

18 slices day-old French bread

3 tablespoons butter, softened

18–36 anchovy fillets, washed and drained if salted, drained if packed in oil

12 or so Italian parsley leaves, chopped (optional)

Spread the slices of bread with the butter and top with one or two anchovies; sprinkle on the chopped parsley if you like.

VARIATIONS:

The butter and anchovies can be mashed together and then spread on the bread; the parsley can be incorporated or sprinkled on top.

ROASTED RED PEPPER SPREAD FOR CROUTONS OR CROSTINI

6 servings

2 meaty red bell peppers, roasted, peeled, and seeded

1 teaspoon fresh oregano leaves or ¼ teaspoon dried

2 cloves garlic, peeled

½ cup pitted green or black olives

Crushed hot red pepper flakes

1 tablespoon capers

Balsamic vinegar

Freshly ground black pepper

10–12 slices white or whole-wheat French or Italian bread or 4–6 slices country- or Tuscan-type bread

Extra-virgin olive oil

I use large green Sicilian olives for this, but just about any good-quality olives will bring tasty results.

Place the peppers, oregano, 1 small clove garlic, olives, and hot red pepper into the bowl of a food processor. Pulse to produce a very rough-textured but homogenous mixture; add the capers, a few drops of the vinegar, and pepper to taste, and pulse one or two times more.

Grill or toast the bread. Cut the remaining clove of garlic in half and rub the cut side over the toasted bread; brush the bread slices lightly with olive oil and spread with the pepper mixture.

SHRIMP TOAST

4–6 servings

One or two of these, set next to a small salad, makes for a very tasty first course; cut into small triangles or rounds, they can be served as hors d'oeuvres with cocktails or white wine. Red tomatoes alone can be used, but yellow ones will intensify the pretty coral color of the saffron-shrimp mixture.

Several saffron threads

2 tablespoons white wine

1 tablespoon olive oil

¼ cup minced red onion

1 small clove garlic, peeled and minced

1 jalapeño pepper, seeded and minced

½ cup red or mixed red and yellow small cherry or pear tomatoes

1 pound raw shrimp, shelled and rinsed

1½ tablespoons mayonnaise

2 tablespoons chopped Italian parsley leaves

1 tablespoon capers, drained if in vinegar, washed and drained if salted

10–12 slices French baguette, sliced about ¼ inch thick, or any finely textured white sandwich bread

Place the saffron threads in a small bowl with the wine and let them steep.

Pour the oil into a medium-size skillet over medium-high heat; add the onion, garlic, and jalapeño pepper and sauté, stirring, for a minute or two.

Add the tomatoes and continue to cook, stirring, until the tomatoes begin to break down. Add the shrimp to the pan. The shrimp should cook thoroughly but quickly and the excess moisture should evaporate from the pan as you stir; raise the heat if necessary. Turn the mixture into a mixing bowl and let it cool to room temperature. On a cutting board or in the bowl of a food processor, chop or process the mixture to a rough paste. Stir in the mayonnaise, parsley, and capers.

Toast the bread and spread it with the shrimp mixture.

TUSCAN CHICKEN LIVER CROSTINI

6 servings

Crostini is what the Italians call canapés. Even a casual visitor to Tuscany will learn immediately that there the word is almost interchangeable with pieces of the local bread spread with a paste made of chicken livers.

1 pound chicken livers

¼ cup olive oil

2 tablespoons butter

1 clove garlic, peeled and roughly chopped

6 sage leaves, chopped

Salt

Freshly ground pepper

½ cup chicken broth

2 anchovy fillets, washed and drained if salted, drained if packed in oil (optional)

Lemon juice (optional)

24 small slices day-old Tuscan-type bread

Neighborhood trattorias may offer a rustic version on fairly thick, generous slices of bread, while elegant restaurants will make theirs on smaller, thinner pieces, but in any case, this is a much-loved regional specialty.

Trim the livers of any fat or veins. Place the oil and butter in a medium-size skillet over medium heat; add the garlic and sage and cook for a few minutes without browning. Add the chicken livers to the pan and cook, turning every few minutes just until they have lost their raw color. Add a pinch of salt, pepper to taste, and the broth. Raise the heat slightly and cook, stirring, until the livers are cooked through and most of the broth has evaporated, about 5 minutes.

Place the mixture in the bowl of a food processor along with the anchovies (if using) and pulse several times to form a rough-textured paste; do not puree. Taste and adjust the salt and pepper if necessary and add a few drops lemon juice if you like. Spread the liver paste on the bread and serve.

VARIATIONS:

A tablespoon or so of capers may be added to the puree.

Juniper berries are often added to the mixture as it cooks, and they add a lovely, aromatic edge to the rich flavor. Remove them before pureeing.

I have seen several recipes for this dish that include Marsala wine. I suspect that this worthy ingredient is generally included in chicken liver pâtés from other regions or wandered in as the Tuscan dish became widely popular outside its region.

TOMATO CROSTINI

6 servings

Nearly as ubiquitous in Tuscany as those made with chicken livers are crostini with chopped tomatoes and herbs. One often sees *"crostini misti"* on restaurant menus, which as likely as not turns out to be two of chicken liver and two with tomatoes. This also is a nice way to start a meal at home. The crostini can be served at the table or passed with aperitifs.

This is a dish worthy of your best olive oil.

2 large ripe tomatoes

Salt

Freshly ground pepper

½ cup Italian parsley leaves

10 large basil leaves or 6 mint leaves

⅓ cup plus 1 tablespoon extra-virgin olive oil

6 large slices day-old Tuscan-type bread cut in half or 12–18 slices day-old French bread

Cut the tomatoes in half horizontally and squeeze out the seeds. Chop the tomatoes fairly finely and place them in a bowl with a big pinch of salt and several grindings of pepper. Coarsely chop the herbs, add them to the tomatoes, and stir in ⅓ cup oil.

Brush the remaining oil on the bread and divide the tomato mixture among the slices.

CHEDDAR-SAGE TOAST

6 servings

6–8 slices day-old rye bread, ½ inch thick

2 cups coarsely grated Cheddar cheese

1½ teaspoons Dijon mustard

6 small sage leaves, minced

1 tablespoon butter

I used an English farmhouse Cheddar, sharp but with a somewhat creamy texture that produced excellent results. Look for similar qualities in the cheese you choose. Other breads are fine for this but I prefer rye, wheat, or multi-grain.

Preheat the broiler.

Toast the bread lightly on both sides. Put the cheese, mustard, and sage in a small bowl and combine well. Lightly butter the bread on one side and place the slices, butter side up, on a baking sheet. Divide the cheese mixture among the slices and place under the broiler until the cheese is bubbling and lightly browned—a few minutes, depending on your broiler.

VARIATION:

Lay thin slices of tomato over the butter before covering with the cheese.

Mozzarella in Carrozza

4 servings

This Neapolitan dish is known throughout Italy and beyond, possibly because it is devilishly good. These can be cut into bite-size pieces to serve with aperitifs.

8 thick slices day-old white country-type bread or good-quality white sandwich bread

8 ounces fresh mozzarella or buffalo mozzarella cheese, sliced

½ cup milk

½ cup flour

Salt

Pepper

4 eggs

Olive oil

Place four slices of bread on a work surface, divide the cheese over them, and cover with the remaining bread. Pour the milk into a shallow bowl. On a piece of foil or waxed paper, season the flour with the salt and pepper. Break the eggs into a shallow bowl and beat them lightly.

Holding the sandwiches together, carefully dip them into the milk to coat them lightly, then dredge them in the flour; brush or shake off excess flour. Finally, dip the sandwiches into the eggs.

Place a large heavy skillet over moderate heat. Pour in olive oil to a depth of about ¼ inch. Slip in the sandwiches and fry them, turning once, until they are golden brown on both sides; serve at once.

Toasted Caprese Sandwiches

Caprese salad, named for its origins on the island of Capri, is one of those dishes that defines its season: It is a summer standard on menus throughout Italy and well beyond. And one never tires of it—if, that is, the simple ingredients are all first-rate. Here the Caprese is translated into a pan-grilled sandwich that makes a swell lunch and is even more delightful if cut into pieces and served with drinks before a summer dinner—outdoors if possible.

FOR EACH SANDWICH:

1 thick slice fresh mozzarella or buffalo mozzarella cheese

1 large or 2 small basil leaves

1 thin slice ripe tomato

2 slices pain de mie, Pullman, or other good-quality white sandwich bread, cut ¼ inch thick

Olive oil

Heat a griddle or cast-iron skillet over medium-high heat. Sandwich the mozzarella, basil, and tomato between the slices of bread and lightly brush the outsides with oil. Place the sandwiches in the skillet and cook until evenly golden brown on both sides. Press the sandwiches lightly with a spatula as they cook. Place the sandwiches on a board and cut into strips or triangles.

CRISPS

A crisp is not the same thing as toast. It must be slowly dried out, rather than toasted, so that it can be kept. The bread should acquire very little, if any, color as it achieves its dry, crisp state. Virtually any kind of bread can be turned into crisps. Plain white or country breads are obvious candidates and are useful with just about any topping. Rye, whole-wheat, multi-grain, and pumpernickel as well as pita and Indian breads are especially good for spicy dips, herb butters, and cheese spreads. Otherwise, think of a crisp as a cracker or a chip.

Preheat the oven to 250°. Use a good serrated knife to cut very thin slices from your loaves. Place the bread directly on the oven racks and bake for 30 minutes to an hour; not all breads will dry at the same speed. If you prefer, you can do this on baking sheets, but you will need to turn the slices at the midway point; the total time may be slightly longer.

Spreads and Dips for Crisps

The following casual recipes represent just some of the possibilities. In time you will develop your own combinations. The only rules are that the topping be tasty and that it be of a consistency to remain on the crisp until it reaches the mouth. (See also the toppings for Bruschette and Crostini, and don't forget your own favorite tuna, egg, salmon, or crab-meat salads.)

Pesto

About 1½ cups

1 cup basil leaves
¼–⅓ cup olive oil
¼ cup grated Parmigiano Reggiano cheese
1 clove garlic, peeled
2 tablespoons pignoli (pine nuts)
Freshly ground pepper
Salt

Place the basil and ¼ cup of the oil into the bowl of a food processor and pulse just to blend; add the remaining ingredients, except the salt. Pulse to achieve a semismooth consistency, adding additional oil as desired. Taste and add salt if needed.

AIOLI

About 1 cup

ine on its own as a dip or spread, this important garlic mayonnaise is indispensable to Aioli Monstre, a Provençal feast that features salted cod. Spread Aioli on toasted country bread or Crostini and either float it on seafood soups and stews or place the slices in the dish and then ladle the soup over them.

6–8 cloves garlic, peeled

1 egg yolk

½ teaspoon Dijon mustard

1 cup light olive oil or half olive, half safflower or sesame oil

Pinch saffron

Freshly ground white pepper

Lemon juice

Place the garlic, egg yolk, and mustard in the bowl of a food processor and process to a smooth mixture. With the machine running, add the oil drop by drop; when the mixture begins to emulsify, increase the flow to a thin steady stream. Add the saffron and pepper and lemon juice to taste; thin the sauce to the desired consistency with 1 or 2 teaspoons lukewarm water. Store Aioli in a glass jar in the refrigerator.

ANCHOVY SAUCE

About 1½ cups

Mash or blend in a food processor 4–6 anchovies, 10 (or more) cloves garlic, 1 cup olive oil, 1 cup basil or parsley leaves, and black pepper and red wine vinegar or lemon juice to taste.

Salsa

About 2 cups

2 cups fresh ripe roughly chopped
    tomatoes

½ small red onion, roughly chopped

½ cup (or to taste) cilantro leaves

Hot red or green pepper sauce

Red wine vinegar or freshly squeezed
    lime juice

Salt

Place the tomatoes and onion in the bowl of a food processor and pulse to chop to a chunky consistency. Add the cilantro and hot pepper sauce, vinegar, and salt to taste and pulse just to combine; do not let the mixture become too smooth. Store in a glass container.

Tapenade

About 1¼ cups

1 cup pitted black olives

2 anchovies

4 tablespoons drained capers

1 clove garlic, peeled

Crushed hot red pepper flakes

¼ cup parsley leaves

3–4 tablespoons olive oil

Place all the ingredients except the olive oil in the bowl of a food processor and pulse to finely chop. With the machine running, pour in the oil by tablespoons just until a rough-textured mixture is produced.

Tuna Tapenade

About 2 cups

Add one 6½- or 7-ounce can (they vary) tuna packed in olive oil, drained, to the basic Tapenade.

Olive Spreads

Good-quality green and black olive purees can be found in specialty food markets and many supermarkets. Use them as they are or add capers, minced hot or roasted sweet peppers, grated lemon zest, crushed hot red pepper flakes, or chopped fresh herbs.

Cream Cheese Spreads

About 1½ cups

Mix 8 ounces of cream cheese with ¼ pound minced smoked salmon, 1 tablespoon lemon juice, and 1 teaspoon chopped chives or dill; 2 chopped scallions; or 8–10 minced black or green olives.

Flavored Butters

About 1 cup

8 ounces butter, softened, with any of the following:

2 tablespoons minced shallots

chopped parsley, chives, chervil, tarragon, cilantro

Dijon mustard

minced jalapeño pepper

chili powder, ground cumin, coarsely ground pepper

lemon juice, red wine vinegar

Whisk or beat the butter until it is fluffy. Add any of the ingredients listed, alone or in combinations.

BREAD SALADS

Bread salads fall into two general categories. The first, oldest, and most traditional are made with stale bread that is resuscitated with water or water and vinegar and then combined with other ingredients and dressed. The Italian panzanella is a typical salad made with soaked stale bread. The second category includes dried croutons as one of the ingredients that are dressed and tossed together; the ubiquitous Caesar salad is the foremost example here.

MY CAESAR SALAD

—

PANZANELLA

—

PAPA'S BREAD SALAD

—

CAPER BERRY AND RYE BREAD SALAD

—

ASPARAGUS AND BREAD SALAD WITH ASIAN FLAVORS

—

CORN BREAD CHICKEN SALAD

—

SOUTHWESTERN STEAK AND CORN BREAD SALAD

—

DAY-OLD FOCACCIA SALAD

My Caesar Salad

4–6 servings

No collection of dishes including bread could omit this American classic. The legend has been told often enough—Caesar Cardini invented the dish at his restaurant, Caesar's Place, in Tijuana, Mexico. Over the years it has become axiomatic that the inclusion of anchovies was essential, but according to food writer John Mariani, this was not the case, and in his *The Dictionary of American Food and Drink*, he presents the original recipe to prove it. For me, however, anchovies are an important feature of a Caesar salad.

As popular and widespread as Caesar salad now is, a really good execution is rare. Most include far too much garlic along with inferior Parmigiano cheese. In addition, a reasonable fear of salmonella has led virtually all restaurants and many home cooks to omit Cardini's coddled eggs from the dressing. When I make Caesar salad at home, I sometimes include the undercooked eggs and take my chances, but I have also come to love this version with hard-cooked eggs. It is a favorite when I enjoy the novelty of dining alone. Use more or fewer eggs depending on the number of servings and if the salad is to precede a meal or be its main course.

In the spirit of full disclosure I must add that my preference is for frisée or the inner leaves of chicory (curly endive) rather than romaine lettuce, but that takes the dish too far from the original to even be a variation.

*2–3 slices good white bread, a day
    or more old*

2 heads romaine lettuce

⅓ cup good-quality olive oil

1 clove garlic, peeled and crushed

Salt

Juice of ½ lemon

*4–6 anchovy fillets, rinsed and
    dried if salted, drained on paper
    towels if packed in oil*

Freshly ground pepper

*¼ cup grated Parmigiano
    Reggiano cheese*

2–4 hard-cooked eggs

Cut the bread into ½-inch cubes; you should have about 2 cups. If the bread is at all soft, dry it out in a 350° oven, but do not toast it. Discard any tough or bruised outer leaves of the romaine, then cut the leafy part away from the ribs. Wash the leaves, drain them well, and wrap them in paper towels or a kitchen towel to dry thoroughly.

Put 2 tablespoons of the oil into a large heavy skillet over medium heat. Add the garlic and cook it briefly, just until it begins to color. Add the bread and cook, stirring, until the cubes are as uniformly golden brown as possible, but do not let them burn or become very dark. Remove the bread from the pan and sprinkle it lightly with salt. Discard the garlic.

Pour the remaining oil into the bowl from which you will serve the salad; add the lemon juice and whisk to combine. Add the anchovies and mash them lightly with a fork; season generously with the pepper. Place the romaine in the bowl and toss thoroughly to coat the leaves well. Sprinkle the cheese over and toss again briefly. Crumble the eggs over the salad, sprinkle the croutons over, and serve.

VARIATION:

If you wish to make the original coddled-egg dressing, bring a small pot of water to a boil, carefully lower two eggs in, and, when the water returns to the boil, cook the eggs for exactly 2 minutes. Remove the eggs, crack them into the dressing, and whisk to incorporate well.

PANZANELLA

6 servings

The renowned Tuscan bread salad is now routinely found throughout Italy, as well as in the United States, though not always well presented. A friend recently disparaged panzanella to me, referring to it as "wet bread." This should not be the reaction to this delightful dish; the fault could lie with using a too-mushy bread or with failing to squeeze enough moisture from it following the soaking; clearly, these errors are easy enough to avoid.

The recipe below is more or less traditional, and the one I always make. Variations can be found from place to place, even in Italy, and to me they all are legitimate if not necessarily authentic, but to my taste, some restraint should be exercised, and only a few ingredients included. I have enjoyed versions with anchovies, cucumbers, scallions, capers, olives, tuna, and hard-cooked eggs—but not all in the same panzanella.

Bread, tomato, and basil are the constants, and there is no point in making this unless you have at hand ripe summer tomatoes and some facsimile of good Tuscan bread.

The method of covering the salad with plastic wrap for a short time before dressing and serving comes from Giuliano Bugialli and it is a step worth taking to help merge the salad's flavors.

1 pound Tuscan bread or similar, sturdy country bread, whole-wheat if possible, several days old

2 medium red onions

2 pounds ripe red tomatoes

2–3 stalks celery from the heart, leaves included, trimmed and washed

½ cup basil leaves plus additional for the garnish

¾ cup extra-virgin olive oil

¼ cup red wine vinegar

Salt

Freshly ground pepper

Cut or tear the bread up into large chunky pieces and place them in a large bowl. Cover the bread well with water—4 or more cups. Let the bread soak for about 30 minutes.

Peel the onions and cut them in half lengthwise, then into very thin crosswise slices. Place the onions in the dish from which you will serve the salad. Cut the tomatoes into chunky pieces. Roughly chop the celery. Add the tomatoes and celery to the dish.

Squeeze as much water as you can from the bread and place it over the ingredients in the dish; tear the ½ cup basil leaves into pieces and distribute it over the bread. Cover the dish with plastic wrap and refrigerate for 30 minutes.

Remove the dish from the refrigerator; if it seems very cold, let it sit for 10 minutes. Whisk together the oil and vinegar and salt and pepper to taste and pour the dressing over the salad. Mix to combine the ingredients very well; taste and adjust as necessary with salt, pepper, and vinegar—you may even want to add a bit more oil. Decorate the panzanella with additional basil and serve at once.

VARIATION:

The vinegar can be added to the water used to soak the bread, in which case it should be eliminated from the dressing.

Papa's Bread Salad

4 servings

My grandfather loved this dish, which was made with bread that was intentionally produced to be hard so that it would keep without spoiling; it still can be found in Italian groceries, labeled *frisella* or *"pan biscotto"*—twice-baked. I favor the whole-wheat type made with cracked black pepper (*biscotti di pepe*). Very stale Italian whole-wheat bread can be substituted; dry it out in a slow oven for about 10 minutes if necessary. To approximate the taste of *biscotti di pepe*, I use a copious amount of pepper.

4 thick slices hard whole-wheat bread

½ cup olive oil

1 small clove garlic, peeled and minced

3 tablespoons red wine vinegar

Salt

Cracked or coarsely ground pepper

1 small red onion, thinly sliced

Young dandelion greens or arugula, washed, dried, and torn into pieces to produce 2–3 cups, loosely packed

1 cup chopped ripe tomatoes

2 hard-cooked eggs, quartered (optional)

Place the bread in a bowl, cover well with lukewarm water, and set aside for 30 minutes or so—the bread should completely sponge up the water.

Meanwhile, in your serving dish, whisk together the olive oil, garlic, vinegar, and a pinch of salt and pepper to taste. Toss in the onion.

When the bread is ready, squeeze out as much excess water as possible, tear it up, add it to the dish, and toss. Add the greens and the tomatoes, toss again, top with the eggs, and serve.

VARIATIONS:

Papa's salad was subject to whim. Anchovies are a natural addition; other greens, including basil, can be used, and cucumbers, fennel, and capers can be added.

CAPER BERRY AND RYE BREAD SALAD

8 servings

Caper berries are beginning to be widely distributed. Try to find them, but if you cannot, large capers can be substituted. I leave the stems on for this salad, but remove them if you like. Just about any bread can be used, but the taste of rye has a nice affinity for the caper berries. This is a great starter salad; it also is a marvelous accompaniment to gravlax or other types of cured salmon.

4 cups dry rye bread cut into ½-inch cubes

1 teaspoon Dijon mustard

4 tablespoons champagne or white wine vinegar

⅓ cup olive oil

Pinch sea salt or coarse salt

Freshly ground white or black pepper

4 scallions, trimmed and sliced (white part plus about 1 inch of green tops)

2 cucumbers

1 bunch (about 10) red or white radishes, washed, trimmed, and thinly sliced

⅔ cup caper berries

1½ cups Italian parsley leaves

If the rye bread cubes are not completely dry, toast them in a 350° oven for about 10 minutes or in a large skillet over medium heat.

Whisk together the mustard, vinegar, and olive oil and season to taste with salt and pepper in a large salad bowl. Toss the bread cubes with the dressing, then with the scallions.

Peel the cucumbers if they are waxed. Cut them in half lengthwise and remove the seeds using a teaspoon or melon baller. Cut the shells crosswise into slices about ¼ inch thick. Toss the cucumbers, radishes, caper berries, and parsley with the ingredients in the bowl and serve at once.

ASPARAGUS AND BREAD SALAD WITH ASIAN FLAVORS

4–6 servings

1 stalk lemongrass

1½-inch piece of gingerroot

4 tablespoons safflower or light sesame oil

4 tablespoons dark sesame oil

6 tablespoons rice wine vinegar

4 tablespoons soy sauce

3–4 drops green jalapeño sauce (optional)

1 pound slim or medium asparagus

Salt

2 tablespoons sesame seeds

4 loose cups mizuna or watercress leaves, washed and patted dry

3 cups dry semolina, whole-wheat, multi-grain, or country-style white bread cut into ½-inch cubes

Mizuna is a one of the Asian greens that have become available and popular in the last year or so; it looks a bit like an overgrown Italian parsley leaf with feathery, pointy edges. You may already have encountered it in a mesclun mix.

Cut the bulb end of the lemongrass off the stalk and discard the tough dark top or keep it for broth. Trim away the tough outer leaves from the bulb and mince it very finely. Peel the gingerroot and mince it. Whisk together the oils, vinegar, soy sauce, and jalapeño sauce. Set the dressing aside.

Place a medium-size pot of water over high heat. Snap off the tough ends of the asparagus and peel the stalks if this seems necessary. Cut the asparagus on the diagonal into pieces about 1½ inches long; set the tips aside. When the water reaches the boil, add a large pinch of salt and the asparagus stalks; when the water returns to the boil cook the asparagus for 1 to 2 minutes—they should remain crisp. Quickly drain the asparagus and refresh them under cold water. Drain well, pat dry, and place, along with the tips, in your serving dish.

Place the sesame seeds in a small skillet over medium heat. Stirring constantly, cook the seeds until they are lightly toasted and golden in color—take care not to let the seeds become too dark or they will have a burned, bitter taste. Remove the seeds from the pan immediately.

If the bread is not quite dry, toast it in the oven or in a large skillet over medium heat. Pour the dressing over the asparagus, add the mizuna and bread, and toss together to combine. Scatter the sesame seeds over the salad and serve.

VARIATION:

Cooked small or medium shrimp can be substituted for the asparagus, or added to make a substantial but light main-course salad.

Corn Bread Chicken Salad

4–6 servings

Kernels from 2 ears fresh corn or
  1 cup frozen and defrosted

Salt

½ cup buttermilk

¼ cup mayonnaise, plain yogurt,
  or sour cream

2 teaspoons Dijon mustard

1 tablespoon white wine vinegar

¼ cup snipped chives

Freshly ground white pepper

2 cups corn bread cut into 1-inch
  cubes and lightly toasted in the
  oven

10–12 cherry tomatoes, cut in half,
  or 2 large tomatoes, cut into
  thin wedges

Leaves from 1 bunch watercress,
  washed and dried

2 cups sliced cooked chicken
  (roasted, grilled, or broiled)

Bring a small pot of water to a boil, add a pinch of salt and the corn. Boil for 1 minute, then quickly refresh the corn under cold water and drain it well.

In your serving dish, whisk together the buttermilk, mayonnaise, mustard, vinegar, and chives; season to taste with salt and pepper. Add the corn bread to the dressing and toss; set aside for about 10 minutes. Add the tomatoes, watercress, chicken, and corn and toss well before serving.

Variations:

Diced jicama, avocado, or roasted red peppers, or sliced blanched green beans, can be substituted for the corn or added to the salad. One quarter pound of baked ham or crisp bacon can also be added.

SOUTHWESTERN STEAK AND CORN BREAD SALAD

3–4 main-course servings

1 pound boneless shell steak

2–3 cups dry day-old corn bread cut into 1-inch cubes

1 ripe avocado

Juice of ½ lemon

Salt

Freshly ground black pepper

½ cup olive or vegetable oil

2 tablespoons red wine vinegar

1 jalapeño pepper, seeded and minced

About 4 dashes red or green hot pepper sauce, or to taste

1 pound cherry or cocktail tomatoes, halved or quartered, depending on their size

1 small head crisp lettuce, such as romaine, washed and torn into pieces

This is substantial enough for a main course. Corn on the cob or black beans are perfect side dishes. If you make the bread with this dish in mind, advance the Southwestern aspect by adding to the batter 1 minced fresh or canned jalapeño pepper, ¼ cup minced onion, and 1 tablespoon chili powder or ground cumin. Grilled pork or chicken can replace the beef.

Grill or broil the steak to rare or medium rare. If the bread is not dry, toast it in the oven.

Roughly mash the avocado with the lemon juice and season to taste with salt and pepper. Whisk together the oil, vinegar, minced jalapeño pepper, and hot pepper sauce. Place the bread cubes, tomatoes, and dressing in a shallow serving bowl or deep platter and toss together; let the mixture sit for 5–10 minutes. Just before serving, slice the steak on a slight diagonal about ¼ inch thick. Toss the bread mixture with the lettuce and top with the avocado mixture and the steak slices.

Day-Old Focaccia Salad

4–6 servings

One day old or five days old hardly matters—focaccia past its prime is a grim prospect. Its chewy texture, however, makes it a marvelous candidate for a second life in a salad. This one is a kind of tomato-free panzanella, certainly open to wide interpretation. I used a rather plain focaccia—herbs and salt, no cheese, no meat, no vegetables, but just about any type will do.

About 3 cups broken stale focaccia

6 tablespoons red wine vinegar

¾ cup olive oil

1 tablespoon lemon juice, or more to taste

Freshly ground black pepper

1 clove garlic, peeled and finely minced

4 anchovies, rinsed and drained if salted, drained if packed in oil

½ red onion, peeled and thinly sliced

1 small fennel bulb

1 small head frisée or inner leaves of chicory or escarole, broken into bite-size pieces and washed and drained well

2 endive, cleaned and sliced crosswise

⅓ cup small black olives such as Niçoise or Gaeta, pitted and cut in half

Place the focaccia in a large bowl and cover generously with water (about 4 cups); add the vinegar and mix to combine. Let the bread soak for about 30 minutes.

In your serving dish, whisk together the olive oil, lemon juice, and pepper to taste. Add the garlic and anchovies; mash the anchovies into the dressing to break them up. Add the onion to the dressing. When the bread is ready, squeeze out the excess water and toss the bread with the other ingredients.

Trim the tough, outer layers from the fennel and slice the bulb thinly, crosswise. Snip off some of the feathery fennel tops and add them, with the sliced bulb, to the dish. Add the frisée and the endive to the salad, toss everything well, and top with the olives.

BREAD SOUPS

Soup seems to have been the earliest approach to making good use of stale bread—that is, if a dish achieved by pouring water onto hard bread, as the Romans did, can be considered soup. Simple additions like herbs and olive oil made the concoctions more palatable, and in time a category of soup so large that it could fill a book by itself had been developed. In our more affluent times, broth often replaces water, but many of the old soups survive in the home cook's repertoire thanks to their ease of preparation and thriftiness, and, not incidentally, their goodness.

GAZPACHO

WHITE GAZPACHO

ACQUACOTTA

PAPPA AL POMODORO

ONION SOUP

AÇORDA

EGG AND BREAD CRUMB SOUP

RIBOLLITA

ANOTHER RIBOLLITA

GARLIC BREAD SOUP

GARLIC BREAD SOUP #2

SPRING SOUP WITH GOAT CHEESE TOASTS

BLACK BEAN TORTILLA CHILI

FARRO-MUSHROOM SOUP WITH CHEESE TOASTS

ZUPPA PAVESE

GAZPACHO

4–6 servings

It comes as a big surprise to many that not only did gazpacho exist before the tomato had found its way to Spain, but that it goes all the way back to ancient times. If gazpacho was not the first soup, it was one of the first, and an early example of the impulse to recycle stale bread. For a full discussion of gazpacho, I refer you to Raymond Sokolov's *Why We Eat What We Eat*, a smart and lively study of the post-Columbian food exchange.

I must confess that, while I like the concept of gazpacho, I am often disappointed in its execution, especially in restaurants. Sometimes canned tomato juice is the base for too many ingredients that are simply ground up into it. For a tomato-based gazpacho, which is to say gazpacho by today's definition, nothing short of delicious ripe tomatoes is acceptable. In addition, gazpacho usually is served too cold for my taste. Curiously—since it is historically a bread-based soup—gazpacho often is breadless; sometimes, even the ubiquitous tough little packaged croutons are missing from the garnish.

This is a relatively simple and typical Spanish gazpacho, which I serve at cool room temperature, in the traditional way. The obvious appeal of all good gazpachos aside, the food processor must be given some credit for the popularity of this dish today; what once was arduously pounded by hand can now be deftly executed with the push of a button.

2–4 pieces stale sturdy white
    sandwich bread, French bread,
    or Swiss peasant-style or other
    rustic white bread

2 pounds ripe tomatoes

1 green bell pepper

1 red bell pepper

1 cucumber

1 small sweet or red onion

3 (or more) cloves garlic

¾ cup extra-virgin olive oil

⅓ cup white wine vinegar

2 tablespoons sherry vinegar

Salt

Freshly ground pepper

GARNISHES:

Chopped tomato, cucumber, green
    pepper, chopped hard-cooked eggs,
    fried coarse bread crumbs
    (optional)

Place the bread in a large bowl, pour in water to cover, and let the bread soak for about 30 minutes.

Cut the tomatoes in half horizontally and squeeze out the seeds. Remove the stems and seeds from the peppers and cut them into pieces. Peel the cucumber, cut it in half, and with a teaspoon or melon baller, scoop out the seeds. Cut the cucumbers into ¼-inch slices, and peel and roughly chop the onion and garlic.

Place the vegetables in the bowl of a food processor and process to a fairly smooth consistency. Squeeze the bread as thoroughly as you can and add it to the puree; process again, and, while the machine is running, slowly pour the oil and vinegars through the tube. Add cold water, a cup or more, until you achieve the desired consistency—the soup should be very smooth and medium thick. Add salt and pepper to taste and additional vinegar as necessary. Serve at once or chill the soup slightly.

Arrange whichever of the garnishes you choose on a plate or in small dishes and pass them at the table.

WHITE GAZPACHO

6 servings

In truth, this soup is pale green and far from authentic, but it is lovely.

4–6 slices stale good-quality white sandwich bread or French bread

2 slender zucchini

4 cloves garlic

3 shallots

1 cucumber

1 head Boston lettuce or other soft lettuce

1 cup Italian parsley leaves

2 tablespoons cilantro, mint, basil, or chervil leaves

¼ cup pignoli (pine nuts) or almonds

½ cup extra-virgin olive oil

3 tablespoons white wine vinegar

2 tablespoons sherry vinegar

1 cup light defatted chicken or vegetable broth

Salt

Freshly ground white pepper

Place the bread in a bowl and pour in water to cover.

Scrub the zucchini and shred them coarsely by hand or in a food processor. Drain the zucchini and place it, with ¼ cup water, in a small skillet over medium heat; cover and steam for 2 minutes. Place the zucchini in a strainer, refresh it under cold water, and drain it well.

Peel the garlic cloves and shallots. Peel the cucumber, cut it in half horizontally, and with a teaspoon or melon baller, remove the seeds; cut the cucumber into chunks. Trim the lettuce and discard any tough or bruised leaves; discard the tough ribs and tear the leaves into large pieces.

Place the garlic, shallots, cucumber, parsley, cilantro, and pignoli into the bowl of a food processor and process until fairly smooth.

Squeeze as much liquid as you can from the bread and add it to the ingredients in the bowl. With the machine running, pour the oil and vinegars through the feed tube. Pour in the broth and process until smooth. Add the reserved zucchini and the lettuce and process just to combine and create a semirough texture. Season to taste with salt and pepper and add small amounts of cold water if necessary to achieve a semithick consistency.

ACQUACOTTA

6 servings

A very old dish from the peasant cuisine, "cooked water" perseveres, like Pappa al Pomodoro and Ribollita, more for its goodness than out of necessity. Variations abound. The version here is similar to one in Ada Boni's *Il Talismano*, the Italian *Joy of Cooking*. The author's notes suggest it as a good choice for lean, or fast, days.

3 pounds ripe tomatoes

4 onions, thinly sliced

8 fresh mint or basil leaves

Salt

6 slices Tuscan or other rustic bread, whole-wheat if possible, several days old

⅓ cup olive oil

Pepper

Grated Parmigiano Reggiano cheese

Cut the tomatoes in half and squeeze out the seeds. Roughly chop the tomatoes and place them in a saucepan over medium heat with barely enough water to cover; bring just to a boil, lower the heat to a simmer, and cook until the tomatoes are broken down and the liquid has begun to thicken, about 15 minutes.

Add the onions, the mint, and a pinch of salt, partially cover the pot, and continue to simmer until the ingredients resemble a sauce of medium consistency.

If the bread is not quite stale, lay the slices on a baking sheet and place it in a 350° oven to dry but not toast. Place the slices in each of six soup plates and drizzle the olive oil over; season each slice with salt and pepper to taste. Adjust the thickness of the soup if necessary with small amounts of water, reheat, and ladle it over the bread. Sprinkle the cheese over each portion or pass it at the table.

Pappa al Pomodoro

6–8 servings

This version of Tuscany's remarkable tomato and bread soup deviates only proportionally from one by my friend Giuliano Bugialli, the renowned Italian food authority, teacher, and author. I find that mine requires more tomatoes and broth than Giuliano's; the difference may be due to the characteristics of what falls short of real Tuscan bread in even our best bakeries. Use a bread with a heavy crust and tight crumb for this and feel free to make adjustments in the amount of broth you use.

Clearly, tomatoes make this a splendid summer dish, but it should not be eliminated from your winter menus. You can get fine results with the best canned tomatoes available; look for a product that includes tomatoes only, without puree—I especially like the vacuum-packed chopped tomatoes from Italy. This is the time to splurge on a really good virgin olive oil to pass at the table and drizzle over the finished soup.

If the bread is not several days old, or does not seem stale enough, place it on a baking sheet and put it in a preheated 350° oven for 10 minutes or so—the bread should be dry, but not toasted.

Pour the broth into a medium saucepan and bring it to a low boil over medium-high heat.

*1 pound Tuscan-type bread, several
days old, cut into 1-inch cubes
(about 4 cups)*

*7 cups homemade or best-quality store-
bought chicken or meat broth*

4 cloves garlic, peeled

10 large fresh sage leaves

¾ cup olive oil

*3 cups chopped seeded very fresh or
best-quality canned tomatoes*

Salt

Freshly ground black pepper

Extra-virgin olive oil

Finely chop the garlic and sage leaves together. Place the olive oil in a large soup pot over medium heat and add the garlic and sage; sauté, stirring, until they are lightly colored, about 5 minutes. Add the tomatoes and stir to incorporate them well for about 2 minutes. Add up to 6 cups of the boiling broth to the bread mixture—the soup should be very thick. Season to taste with salt and pepper, bring just to a boil, cover, and set aside for at least 1 hour.

Before serving, stir the soup vigorously to break up any lumps of bread and add small quantities of the remaining broth as necessary, still maintaining a thick consistency. Serve the soup at room temperature, or, in winter, slightly warmed if you prefer. Drizzle individual portions with the virgin olive oil as you serve them or pass the oil around the table.

NOTE: This particular pappa is in the style of Livorno. Though bread, garlic, tomatoes, and broth are the consistent elements, other variations abound. Basil, in place of sage, is often the herb of choice, and parsley certainly can be used.

ONION SOUP

8 servings

French onion soup is a dish that has suffered from its popularity. It can be a magnificent creation or a bore, or worse. Too often, the broth is lackluster except for the bitter taste of burned onions, and indifferent cooks using inferior cheese often manage to produce a rubbery seal where a tender blanket of cheese should be. Successful onion soup depends on care in the preparation of its few simple ingredients. The onions must be cooked long and slow, without any sign of burning, to develop their flavor and sweetness, and your average canned beef broth just won't do.

2 tablespoons olive oil

2 tablespoons butter

3 large onions (2 pounds), thinly sliced

2 quarts homemade or good-quality store-bought beef broth

Salt

Sugar

2 tablespoons flour

12 or more thick slices stale French bread

1½ cups grated Parmigiano Reggiano or French Gruyère cheese, or a combination

Place the olive oil and butter in a large heavy pot over moderate heat. When the butter ceases foaming, stir in the onions. Lower the heat, cover the pot, and cook the onions, stirring from time to time, until they are very soft, about 20 minutes.

Meanwhile, bring the broth to a simmer and keep it warm. Stir pinches of salt and sugar into the onions, and continue to cook for about 45 minutes more, until the onions are a rich golden brown color.

Stir the flour into the onions and cook, stirring, for 2 minutes.

Preheat the oven to 350°.

Pour the broth into the onions and simmer for 45 more minutes.

Place the bread on a baking sheet and lightly toast it in the oven. Just before serving, preheat the broiler. Sprinkle the toast with the cheese, place it under the broiler to melt and brown lightly. At the table, ladle the soup into individual bowls and top with the toasts.

VARIATIONS:

The cheese can be omitted and the bread rubbed with garlic; the garlic bread can be floated on top or placed in the dishes before the soup is ladled over.

A tablespoon or two of the cheese can be placed in the bottoms of the soup plates or bowls before the soup is ladled out and topped with the cheese toasts.

The soup can be gratinéed. Preheat the oven to 450°. Pour the soup into an ovenproof tureen, top with the toast and cheese, and transfer to the oven until the cheese is bubbling and lightly browned. Take care not to overcook the cheese or it will toughen.

In Italian versions, fontina cheese is often used.

Two teaspoons fresh thyme, 1 leaf fresh sage, minced, or 1 bay leaf can be added to the simmering soup. Remove the bay leaf before serving.

AÇORDA

2 large or 4 small servings

My friend Manuela Soares passed along her mother's recipe for this traditional Portuguese bread soup with these comments:

"This was the recipe my mother used to make when we were very young and not feeling well . . . this is a very soothing soup with very subtle and very mild flavors. My mother claims that the bay leaf is the secret ingredient, but she can do without the parsley. In other recipes for açorda, and there are many in Portuguese cuisine, cilantro is used instead of parsley. But in my own experience eating my family's cooking and at restaurants—mostly in Lisbon and northern Portugal—cilantro isn't used that much."

Regarding other variations, Manuela has come across an açorda made with coriander and another that includes wheat bread, corn bread, and thyme, and even one with codfish and tomato. In short, garlic, olive oil, and eggs seem to be the constants; after that, the home cook is at liberty to improvise.

3 tablespoons olive oil

2 cloves garlic, peeled and cut in half

2 teaspoons finely minced parsley

1 bay leaf

Salt

½ French baguette, a day or two old

2 eggs

Place the oil, garlic, parsley, bay leaf, and salt to taste in a medium-size heavy-bottomed saucepan; pour in 3½ cups water and place the pan over high heat.

Cut the bread into ½-inch rounds—you should have 25–30 pieces—and toast them. When the soup reaches a boil, stir in the bread, lower the heat to a simmer, and cook for 5–8 minutes; the mixture will seem very thin.

Turn the heat to low. Make a space for the eggs in the bread, then drop the eggs, one by one, into the broth. Simmer over very low heat without stirring for 5–8 minutes longer, depending on the preferred doneness of the eggs. Remove the bay leaf and immediately spoon the soup into bowls; the eggs can be cut in half for four servings.

EGG AND BREAD CRUMB SOUP

6–8 servings

A variation on the egg and bread theme, this one is elegant enough to serve before a simple dinner.

2 quarts chicken, beef, veal, or vegetable broth

4 tablespoons dry bread crumbs

4 eggs

1 cup grated Parmigiano Reggiano cheese

Freshly ground white or black pepper

Minced parsley

Pour the broth into a medium-size saucepan and bring to a low boil over medium-high heat. While it is still on the heat, stir the bread crumbs into the soup, and keep it at a simmer.

Beat the eggs well, then beat in half the cheese and combine well; season with pepper to taste. Pour the egg mixture into a soup tureen or other serving dish. Ladle about 1 cup of the broth into the tureen, whisking all the while, then very slowly pour in the rest of the broth while continuing to whisk. Sprinkle the parsley on the soup and serve it at once; pass the remaining cheese at the table.

RIBOLLITA

6–8 servings

Ribollita in Italian means to reboil, or boil again. Traditionally, leftover vegetable soup was remade with the addition of stale bread, which thickened it and added flavor. As with so many old-fashioned thrift-conscious dishes, ribollita is now much-loved and intentionally made, which means planning a day ahead. Otherwise, it is simple enough, and open to some interpretation by the cook.

Cavolo nero—black cabbage—a very dark green leafy Italian vegetable, is beginning to appear in our markets, sometimes labeled "Tuscan kale," "*Lacinato*," or "Dinosaur kale." It is delicious and worth asking for, but if you cannot find it, simply increase the quantities of cabbage and Swiss chard.

Drain the beans and place them in a large pot. Cut one celery stalk and one carrot into several pieces and add them to the pot with the garlic, prosciutto, and 1 tablespoon of olive oil; pour in about 4 quarts water—enough to generously cover the beans. Place the pot over medium-high heat and when it reaches a slow boil reduce the heat and partially cover the pot. Simmer the beans until they are tender but not soft, about 40 minutes. Drain the beans, discarding the celery, carrot, and garlic, but reserving the cooking water. Refresh the beans under cold water and set them aside.

Meanwhile, chop together the remaining celery, carrots, and the onion and parsley. Heat the remaining oil in a large pot over medium heat and stir in the chopped

8 ounces dried cannellini beans,
  soaked overnight

3 stalks celery, trimmed and washed

3 carrots, peeled

2 cloves garlic, gently smashed
  and peeled

2 ounces prosciutto, pancetta,
  or slab bacon

⅓ cup plus 1 tablespoon olive oil

1 onion

½ cup parsley leaves

2 tablespoons tomato paste

½ teaspoon dried thyme

Salt

Pepper

1 pound cabbage

1 pound Swiss chard

1 pound cavolo nero

1 pound (2 medium) all-purpose
  potatoes

4 cups chicken broth

6–8 slices Tuscan bread,
  several days old

Extra-virgin olive oil

vegetables; cook the vegetables until they are soft but not browned. Stir the tomato paste into the mixture and cook, stirring, for a few minutes longer.

Pour the reserved bean cooking water into the pot and add the thyme and salt and pepper to taste. Bring the liquid to a low boil and simmer for 15 minutes.

Core the cabbage and cut it into shreds. Cut the Swiss chard and *cavolo nero* leaves away from their tough stalks and then into shreds. Rinse the greens. Peel and cube the potatoes. Add the greens, the potatoes, and 2 cups of the broth to the pot and simmer for about 45 minutes longer, adding broth as needed to maintain a thick soup. Add the beans and cook for 5 minutes.

Place a layer of bread in a large bowl or container. Or, do this in another pot if one is available that will fit into your refrigerator. Ladle the soup over the bread, make another layer of bread, and continue, finishing with soup, until everything is used up. Set the soup aside to cool to room temperature, then cover and store in the refrigerator overnight.

Remove the soup from the refrigerator, bring it to room temperature, reheat it over medium heat, and serve it hot. Pass the additional olive oil at the table.

The soup can be thinned to taste with water or additional broth if it has thickened a great deal, but this by no means should be a "loose" soup.

ANOTHER RIBOLLITA

6–8 servings

In this luxurious version, some of the beans are pureed to thicken the soup.

1 pound cannellini beans, soaked overnight

¾ cup olive oil

3 cloves garlic, peeled and chopped

1 onion, peeled and chopped

1 carrot, scraped and chopped

1 stalk celery, trimmed, washed, and chopped

3 leeks, trimmed, sliced thinly cross-wise, and carefully washed

1 tablespoon chopped fresh rosemary

Crushed hot red pepper flakes (optional)

1 meaty smoked ham hock

Salt

Freshly ground black pepper

6–8 slices Tuscan-type bread

¾ cup grated Parmigiano Reggiano cheese

Drain the beans. Place a large pot over medium heat and add ¼ cup of the oil, about half the garlic, the onion, carrot, celery, leeks, rosemary, and a pinch of hot pepper. Slowly sauté the mixture until it is soft but not browned. Add the beans and the ham hock and cover with water. Bring the liquid to a low boil, lower the heat, and simmer until the beans are quite tender, about 45 minutes.

Remove the ham hock. With a slotted spoon, remove about half the beans and place them in the bowl of a food processor with a bit of the liquid. Puree the beans, then return the puree to the pot. If the ham hock retains any taste, remove bits of the meat and return them to the pot; discard the bone and skin. Season the soup with salt and pepper to taste.

Place the remaining oil in a small skillet over medium heat. Add the remaining garlic and sauté, stirring, just until the garlic turns golden; remove the garlic with a slotted spoon and discard it. Pour half the oil into the soup.

Toast the bread and place the slices in the bottom of a second large pot. Cover the bread with half the cheese, then ladle the soup over; top with the remaining cheese and drizzle the oil from the skillet over. Cover and reheat the soup slowly. The soup also may be reheated in the oven in an ovenproof pot or covered casserole.

GARLIC BREAD SOUP

6 servings

This is one of the dishes that defines the creativity of poor cuisines throughout the Mediterranean. The essential elements are garlic, stale bread, olive oil, and water. This version is an old-fashioned Italian one and is the leanest and most basic; chicken, beef, or vegetable broth can be substituted for the water.

4 thick slices sturdy country-style or Tuscan bread, several days old

4 cloves garlic, smashed and peeled

Salt

¼ cup olive oil

½ cup grated Parmigiano Reggiano or pecorino cheese

Place the bread in a medium-size saucepan and pour in 4 cups of water; let the bread and water rest until the water is absorbed, about 15 minutes.

Add the garlic and salt to taste and bring the mixture to a boil over medium heat. Cook, stirring, for 5 minutes. Discard the garlic, stir in the oil, and serve. Top each serving with the cheese.

GARLIC BREAD SOUP #2

6 servings

Like the traditional Italian garlic soup, this Spanish one also was typically made with water but broth is now commonly used. The significant difference is that the garlic is sautéed in the oil, and, usually, the bread is floated on top.

¼ cup olive oil

6–8 garlic cloves, according to taste, peeled

6–8 slices French, or sturdy country-style, or Tuscan bread, ½ inch thick

1½ tablespoons paprika

½ teaspoon cayenne (optional)

1 teaspoon ground cumin

6 cups chicken or beef broth

Several saffron threads

Salt

Heat the oil in a large saucepan, add the garlic, and sauté, stirring, just until the garlic is golden. Using a slotted spoon, remove the garlic from the oil and set it aside. Add the bread to the pan and sauté until it is golden on both sides; set the bread aside.

Off the heat, stir in the paprika, cayenne, and cumin. Pour in the broth, return the soup to the heat, add the saffron, and bring to a low boil. Meanwhile, mash the garlic cloves with a fork and stir them into the soup. Add salt to taste, top the soup with the bread, and serve.

VARIATIONS:

Eggs—one or two per serving—can be poached in the soup following the method for Zuppa Pavese (page 64), or carefully slid into the soup before the bread is placed on top. It is typical to prepare the soup in a fireproof terra-cotta pot and place it in the oven (450°) to cook the eggs.

The bread can be toasted rather than fried.

One-quarter cup (or more) of good Spanish sherry can be added to the soup.

Spring Soup with Goat Cheese Toasts

6 servings

2 slim zucchini

Salt

4 scallions

2 tablespoons butter

6 cups chicken broth

1 head Boston lettuce

½ cup parsley leaves

2 ounces fresh goat cheese at
room temperature

5 tablespoons crème fraîche or
heavy cream

2 tablespoons pignoli (pine
nuts), toasted and chopped

Freshly ground pepper

4 chives, snipped

4 slices day-old pain de mie,
Pullman, or similar good-
quality white slicing bread

Butter or olive oil

Scrub but do not peel the zucchini. Coarsely grate the zucchini and place them in a colander or strainer; add a large pinch of salt, toss well, and set over a bowl to drain.

Trim and wash the scallions and slice them thinly. Place the butter in a large saucepan over moderate heat; when the butter ceases foaming, stir in the scallions. Rinse the zucchini and squeeze out as much excess water as possible, then add the zucchini to the saucepan; cover, lower the heat, and cook for about 2 minutes. Add the broth and bring it to a simmer.

Discard the tough or broken outer leaves from the lettuce and discard the larger ribs. Shred the lettuce finely and add it, with the parsley, to the soup. Simmer gently for 10 minutes, until the vegetables are tender; do not let them overcook.

Meanwhile, beat or whisk the goat cheese to lighten it, then whisk in 3 tablespoons of the crème fraîche; stir in the chopped pignoli, season to taste with pepper, and stir in the chives. Toast the bread to a golden brown color on both sides. Spread lightly with butter and then with the cheese mixture. Cut each slice into three strips.

Remove the soup from the heat and stir in the remaining crème fraîche; check the seasonings and adjust to taste with salt and pepper. Ladle the soup into individual soup plates and float the cheese toasts on top.

Black Bean Tortilla Chili

6 servings

You can manipulate the texture of this delicious chili as you like—soupy or with the usual thickness of chili. In any case the tortillas reflect the common method of thickening chili with cornmeal or masa harina. The underlying corn taste adds great dimension to the other flavors. Any of the traditional garnishes is appropriate: salsa, sour cream, grated Monterey Jack or Cheddar cheese, chopped onions, additional cilantro, along with rice on the side or top.

½ pound dried black beans, soaked overnight

1 bay leaf

1½ teaspoons dried oregano

Crushed hot red pepper flakes

Freshly ground black pepper

1 tablespoon olive or vegetable oil

1 pound ground beef or beef and pork combined

1 cup (1 medium) chopped onion

2 cloves garlic, peeled and minced

1–2 jalapeño or serrano chiles, chopped

1 tablespoon ground dried chile

1 teaspoon ground cumin

26 ounces chopped canned tomatoes

2 cups chicken broth or water

¼ cup full-flavored brewed coffee

6 dry corn tortillas

Drain and rinse the beans and place them in a large saucepan. Cover generously with water and add the bay leaf, ½ teaspoon oregano, a pinch of hot red pepper, and a generous pinch of black pepper. Place the pan over medium-high heat, bring just to a boil, lower the heat, and partially cover. Simmer the beans until tender but still firm, 45 minutes to 1 hour.

Meanwhile, place the oil in a large pot over medium heat. Add the ground meat and cook for about 1 minute, stirring once or twice.

Add the onion, garlic, and chiles and cook until the meat has lost its raw color and the onion and garlic are soft but not browned. Stir in the remaining oregano, ground chili, and cumin. Add the tomatoes, broth, and coffee and cook at a low simmer for 15 minutes.

When the beans are cooked, drain them, reserving the cooking liquid and discarding the bay leaf. Add the beans to the tomato mixture, add about 1 cup of the bean cooking liquid, and simmer for 15 minutes. Break up the tortillas with your hands and add them to the chili. Cover the pan and let the chili sit for 30 minutes or longer. Reheat the chili slowly before serving, adjusting the seasonings and the thickness with additional bean cooking liquid or water.

Farro-Mushroom Soup with Cheese Toasts

6 servings

Farro, an ancient Roman soft wheat, is becoming increasingly available in our markets. I use it so often that it now is as much a staple in my pantry as rice and barley. Some food authorities argue that farro and spelt are the same thing, while others disagree. For the purposes of this soup, it matters not—they can be substituted for each other, as can wheat berries.

This is a seriously hearty dish, perfect for supper on a snowy night. A salad to begin and fresh or poached fruit to end are all you will need.

Bring a large pot of water to the boil; drain the farro and add it to the boiling water; lower the heat and cook at a low boil for 30 to 45 minutes, until the kernels are barely tender. Drain and refresh the farro under cold water.

Place the oil in a large flame- and ovenproof pot or casserole and place it over medium heat. Stir in the farro, the ham hock, and a few grindings of pepper, and pour in 6 cups of broth. Bring the soup just to a boil.

Preheat the oven to 450°.

1½ cups farro, wheat berries, or spelt, soaked in water for 45 minutes

¼ cup plus 1 tablespoon olive oil

1 ham hock, split, or ¼-pound piece of pancetta or slab bacon (optional)

Freshly ground pepper

6 or more cups chicken or vegetable broth or mixture of broth and water

1 stalk celery, cleaned and sliced

3 slender carrots, scraped and sliced about ¼ inch thick

1 large leek, trimmed, sliced, and carefully washed

2 cloves garlic, peeled and crushed

½ pound cremini, shiitake, or white cultivated mushrooms, trimmed and sliced

Salt (optional)

4 slices country bread, whole-wheat if possible

¼ pound Italian fontina cheese, coarsely grated

Add the celery, carrots, leek, and garlic to the pot; lower the heat, cover, and cook for about 15 minutes, until the vegetables are just tender; add the mushrooms and simmer for 5 minutes more. Remove the ham hock and discard it or remove any tasty bits of meat and return them to the soup. Check the seasonings and add salt and pepper if needed and, if the soup seems too thick, additional small quantities of broth or water.

While the soup is cooking, lightly toast the bread on both sides. Remove the pot from the heat and place the bread over the surface of the soup. Distribute the cheese over the slices and place the casserole in the oven. Bake just until the cheese is melted and bubbling and serve at once.

ZUPPA PAVESE

6 servings

This is the best-known dish of Pavia, an ancient northern Italian city also famous for its university and its furriers. Deeply satisfying and comforting, Zuppa Pavese has the virtue of being an easy and cheap balanced dish.

The bread should be a day old, but not hard. The number of slices you need will depend on its width—if you have a narrow baguette, use two slices for each serving; if the bread is 3–4 inches in diameter, one will do. The results depend on your broth, so use homemade or the best store-bought you can find.

2 quarts excellent chicken broth

4 tablespoons butter

6–12 slices French bread, ½ inch thick

6 (or more) eggs

½ cup grated Parmigian Reggiano cheese

Pour the broth into a medium-size pan and bring to a boil. Melt half the butter in a large skillet over medium heat, and, when the foaming subsides, sauté the bread until golden on both sides. Sauté the bread in two batches if necessary and add butter as needed.

Place a slice of bread in each of six soup bowls. Working quickly but carefully, break an egg onto each slice of bread and sprinkle with the cheese. Keeping the broth at a boil, ladle it into each bowl and place a plate over each. The eggs will cook to a soft-boiled stage in the hot broth. Serve immediately.

VARIATION:

This is a little less tricky if you poach the eggs, either separately or in some of the broth before putting them on the bread; they also will become more cooked than by the traditional method.

MAIN DISHES

There is no question that stuffing of one sort or another accounts for the largest category of entree dishes involving bread, and that within the category poultry outnumbers any other candidate. So, here you will find a guide to quantities and ingredients for birds of all sizes with stuffings of many kinds.

Otherwise, bread crumbs make good toppings and crusts that also help to lock in flavor and juices. Pasta is not traditionally considered to be a main dish, but it certainly has achieved that status in contemporary cooking, especially for simple family meals. Here are three examples of pasta dishes made with bread crumbs, which *is* traditional; bread crumbs add texture and taste to pasta, especially in combination with vegetables and, in lean times, were often sprinkled on in place of costly cheese.

BROILED DEVILED CHICKEN

4–6 servings

Two 2½-pound broilers, split, or 4
poussins *or Cornish game hens,
butterflied, washed, and dried*

4 tablespoons olive oil

¼ cup Dijon mustard

1 tablespoon red wine vinegar

2 shallots, minced

1 teaspoon fresh thyme leaves

Salt

Freshly ground pepper

Pinch red pepper flakes, or to taste

*4 cups fresh white or whole-wheat
bread crumbs*

Lemon wedges

This is adapted from Julia Child's Poulets Grillés à la Diable, one of the recipes from *Mastering the Art of French Cooking* that early on became part of my own repertoire. Years later, I developed the variation, putting the basic ingredients under the chicken's skin, which results in a tasty, succulent grilled chicken; for this version, I much prefer small birds, *poussins*, or Cornish game hens.

Preheat the broiler to medium-high.

Brush the chickens with the olive oil, and place them on a pan about 6 inches below the heat. Broil the chickens until they are lightly browned, about 10 minutes on each side, basting from time to time. Remove the pan and pour off and reserve the pan juices.

If the broiler seems very hot, lower it to medium.

Combine the mustard, vinegar, shallots, thyme, salt and pepper to taste, and the red pepper flakes; whisk 2 tablespoons of the pan juices into the mixture. Brush the chickens on both sides with the mustard mixture.

Spread the crumbs on a large sheet of waxed paper and coat the chickens on both sides. Return the chicken to the broiling pan, skin side down, and drizzle with a bit of the remaining juices. Broil until the crumb coating is golden brown but not charred, turn and repeat on the skin side. This will take about 15 minutes longer; the chicken is done when the juices run clear from the thigh. Serve with the lemon wedges.

VARIATION:

Prepare a charcoal fire. Combine 1 tablespoon of olive oil with the mustard, vinegar, shallots, thyme, salt and pepper to taste, red pepper flakes, and 2 cups of bread crumbs. Using your fingers, and starting from the leg ends of the chickens, very gently separate the skin from the flesh beneath it—this is not so tricky as it sounds, but take care not to tear the skin. Divide the bread crumb mixture among the chickens, and insert it under the skin; on the top side, use your fingers to gently push the stuffing around to more or less evenly cover the flesh. Brush the chickens with additional oil and, when the fire is ready, grill them over the coals until nicely browned and the juices from the leg are clear.

SMALL STUFFED BIRDS

The chicken sausage makes these dainty birds substantial enough that one squab or two quail per portion will satisfy even your most famished guest. A good butcher can remove the breast bones, which makes the birds easier to eat.

FOR EACH SERVING

2 teaspoons olive oil

½ shallot, minced

1 small chicken and apple sausage, removed from its casing and broken up

2 shiitake mushroom caps, chopped

2–3 sage leaves, 1 minced

¼ cup large white bread crumbs

Chicken broth as needed

Salt

Freshly ground pepper

1 squab or 2 quail, washed and dried, inside and out

1 thin slice pancetta or ½ slice bacon

Preheat the oven to 400°.

Place half the oil in a skillet over moderate heat. Add the shallot and cook for a minute; add the sausage and cook until it has lost most of its raw color, about 2 minutes, then add the mushrooms and the minced sage. Cook until most of the juices have evaporated. Put the crumbs in a bowl, add the sausage mixture, and stir to combine; add small amounts of chicken broth until the stuffing barely holds together and season to taste with salt and pepper.

Season the cavity of each bird with salt and pepper and pack it loosely with the stuffing; tuck the wings under the body and secure the legs with toothpicks or string. Heat the remaining oil in a skillet over moderate heat. Add the birds and brown them well on all sides. Remove the squabs to a platter, and when cool enough to handle, place first the remaining sage leaves and then the pancetta over the breasts. Place the birds on a rack in a roasting pan and roast for about 15 minutes—the juices should be clear but the flesh should retain some rosy color.

A Guide to Stuffings for Poultry

Chicken, turkey, and other birds are the most popular foods to be filled, and while there are other kinds, bread is overwhelmingly the most familiar stuffing base for them. Here is a basic guide for creating stuffings. Think of this as a formula you can manipulate to your own taste, starting with the quantity of bread recommended for the size of your bird and then adding the embellishments accordingly.

DESIGNING A STUFFING

Once you have settled on the type and amount of bread to use, you will want to flavor your stuffing with other ingredients. In the lists below are excellent choices for bringing taste and moisture to your stuffing and, ultimately, to whatever it goes into. You can regard this almost as a column A and column B situation, and choose one item from each category. You can, of course, choose more than one, but I must caution you against the kitchen sink approach; if you put too many ingredients into your stuffing, you will taste none of them.

As you make your choices, think about the combinations that generally please you, and the tried-and-true ones—corn is good with pork sausages, apples, and sage; mushrooms with pancetta and thyme or rosemary; chestnuts with celery; and so on.

These lists are hardly comprehensive, but they are representative and should lead you to more possibilities.

Sturdy white breads and corn bread—not sweet—are best for poultry, and light whole-wheat can be delicious as well, alone or in combination with white bread. In general, breads with an emphatic sourdough flavor are not good choices.

(continued)

QUANTITIES OF BREAD

For large turkeys (20 or more pounds, plus additional for a casserole): 12 cups

For small turkeys (12–14 pounds): 6 cups

Roasting chicken (5–7 pounds) or whole turkey breasts: 2 cups

For small birds, such as *poussins*, Cornish game hens, squabs: ½–¾ cup each

FRUITS AND VEGETABLES

white, cremini, portobello, shiitake, porcini, or other mushrooms

dried wild mushrooms

apples

pignoli (pine nuts)

chestnuts

celery with leaves

fresh, steamed, or frozen and defrosted spinach

escarole, steamed

cooked wild rice

corn kernels

MEATS, ETC.

pancetta

Italian sweet sausage

ground pork

prosciutto

bacon

chicken or turkey sausage

ground chicken or turkey

vegetable sausages

Parmigiano Reggiano or Romano or other pecorino cheese

ONIONS

shallots

scallions

onions

garlic

leeks

HERBS

parsley

thyme

rosemary

sage

chives

chervil

bay leaves

TO MOISTEN AND ENRICH

butter, melted and cooled

olive or vegetable oil

chicken broth

vegetable broth

milk

ricotta cheese

mascarpone

crème fraîche

heavy cream

plain yogurt

SPICES

pepper—black, white, green, Szechuan

ginger

fennel

paprika

cayenne

ground chile pepper

cumin

cardamom

STUFFING TIPS

If your bread is soft or seems too fresh, dry it in the oven at a low temperature.

All meats should be cooked, usually by sautéing, and drained of excess fat before being incorporated into stuffings. Onions, garlic, and so forth can be sautéed with meat or, after the meat and excess fat are removed, in the same skillet.

Stuffing should be neither too dry nor too moist. Keep in mind that some of the juices and fat from the bird will ooze into the stuffing as the poultry cooks. If your stuffing has meat in it, or ingredients that have been cooked in butter or oil, moisten it further with chicken or vegetable broth. If the stuffing has no other fat, some oil or butter or combination of fat and broth should be used.

Stuffings for large birds like turkeys and roasting chickens can be made predominately of bread, then well seasoned and only modestly garnished with meat. For small birds, particularly squabs and quail, I like to use a heartier stuffing, one with more meat or mushrooms to make the dish more substantial. There are some very good fresh sausages from specialty producers on the market now that broaden the possibilities for stuffings.

Chicken Pot Pie with Leeks

6 servings

Thin slices of French bread spread with shallot butter can replace a pastry or biscuit crust. Serve the toasty bread to the side of the filling.

Place the chicken in a large deep sauté pan or shallow casserole with the parsley, thyme, and one sprig rosemary. Cut one of the shallots in half and add it with a pinch of salt and a few grindings of pepper. Pour in cold water to barely cover the chicken by 1 inch or so. Over medium heat, bring the water just to the boiling point, lower the heat, cover and simmer until the chicken juices run clear at the joints, about 20 minutes. Remove the pan from the heat and let the chicken cool to lukewarm in the liquid.

Skim as much fat as possible from the surface of the chicken poaching liquid. Measure out 4 cups of the liquid and warm it in a small pan.

Finely mince the remaining shallots. Place a medium-size saucepan over moderate heat; add 6 tablespoons of the butter. When the butter has ceased foaming, add half the minced shallots and a pinch of cayenne. Cook briefly, then whisk in the flour. Cook, while continuing to whisk, for about 2 minutes; lower the heat if necessary to prevent sticking or browning. Whisk in the warm chicken broth. Bring the mixture just to a simmer, lower the heat, and cook, stirring from time to time, until it is quite thick, 20 minutes or so. Add salt and pepper to taste.

Preheat the oven to 425°.

One 3–3½-pound chicken

1 whole chicken breast

2 sprigs Italian parsley

2 sprigs thyme

2 sprigs rosemary

3 shallots, peeled

Salt

Freshly ground pepper

10 tablespoons butter

Cayenne

6 tablespoons flour

1 pound (about 16) small new
    potatoes, scrubbed

3 carrots, scraped

1 parsnip, scraped

2 tablespoons olive oil

3 leeks

½ pound shelled peas (from
    1 pound fresh)

2 tablespoons crème fraîche
    or sour cream

1 tablespoon Dijon mustard

¼ pound baked or country ham,
    cubed

About twenty ¼-inch-thick slices
    day-old French baguette

Cut the potatoes in half and the carrots and parsnip into pieces 1½ to 2 inches long. Lightly coat a heavy pan (a cast-iron skillet is perfect for this) with oil and place the potatoes in it, cut side down; scatter the carrot and parsnip pieces around. Drizzle the remaining oil and a pinch of salt over the vegetables; place the pan in the oven and roast the vegetables just until they are tender, 10–15 minutes.

Trim the leeks at the stem end and remove the tough outer layers; cut them in half lengthwise, then crosswise into pieces about 1½ inches wide. Wash the leeks thoroughly, but try to keep the layers together. Place the pieces in a heavy skillet over medium heat, cover, and steam for 2–3 minutes, just long enough to soften them (this also can be done in a plastic wrap–covered dish in a microwave oven). Uncover the leeks and set them aside.

Bring a small pot of water to a boil, add a pinch of salt, and add the peas; cook for 1 minute, drain, and refresh them under cold water.

Soften the remaining butter and stir in the remaining minced shallot, the leaves from the remaining rosemary, finely minced, half the mustard, and a grinding or two of pepper. Spread the butter thinly onto one side of each piece of bread.

(continued)

When the sauce is ready, remove it from the heat and whisk in the crème fraîche and the remaining mustard.

Remove the chicken from its bones in large chunks and cut or tear the breasts apart into similarly sized pieces. Place the chicken and all the vegetables in a large oval or rectangular baking dish that will hold them comfortably; scatter the ham over. Pour the sauce over the ingredients and, with the back of a large spoon, press down gently to level the surface as much as possible. Place the buttered bread over the surface, overlapping the slices slightly; cut the pieces as necessary to fill the gaps.

Loosely, and without disturbing the bread, cover the dish with a sheet of heavy-duty foil. Place it in the oven and cook for about 30 minutes—the bread should just be beginning to brown and the sauce bubbling. Remove the foil and bake for 5–10 minutes longer, until the bread is golden brown. Remove the dish and let it rest for about 5 minutes before serving.

MEATBALLS

4 main-course servings; 6 if served with pasta

Meatballs seem to be out of favor, at least with those who consider themselves to be food sophisticates, and they often are incorrectly disparaged as not being authentically Italian. As far as I am concerned, the only bad meatball is a poorly made one, which comes up too tightly textured and dry. Good meatballs—*polpette* to Italians—are quick and easy; as with most icons of home cooking, they are best if kept simple.

2–3 slices day-old bread

Milk

2 eggs

¼ cup chopped Italian parsley leaves

¼ cup grated Parmigiano Reggiano cheese

Salt

Freshly ground pepper

¾ pound ground beef

½ pound ground veal

Olive oil

Tear the bread into pieces and place it in a small bowl; cover with milk and let soak for about 30 minutes.

Lightly beat the eggs, then stir in the parsley, cheese, a pinch of salt, and a few grindings of pepper. Squeeze and discard the excess milk from the bread and stir the bread into the egg mixture, then add the meat and mix just to combine well; the texture should remain slightly rough. Shape the mixture into meatballs about 2 inches in diameter.

Place a large heavy skillet over moderate heat; pour in oil to a depth of about ¼ inch. When the oil is hot—test by seeing if a small piece of bread sizzles in it—add the meatballs and cook them, turning often until they are golden brown all over. Drain the meatballs on paper towels. Serve at once, or, if you are serving the meatballs with tomato sauce and pasta, warm them in the sauce for about 5 minutes.

 Meatloaf

4 servings

One would be hard-pressed to find a meatloaf recipe that does not include bread crumbs; they are a critical way to lighten as well as bind the meat mixture. When I was growing up in the 1950s, however, an over-abundance of crumbs in the meatloaf meant that the cook was stingy and trying to stretch the meat. Today's cooks are more concerned about health and nutrition and many have reduced the proportion of animal protein in their menus in favor of increased carbohydrates. They also are looking for new ways to fashion traditional dishes.

This meatloaf reflects those interests. The nature of the crumbs themselves is of great importance; these crumbs are large and not bone-dry, in contrast to the pulverized crumbs that defeat the purpose and produce dense, unappealingly compact meatloaves. Here I've also included spinach and tomatoes.

This is a fine meatloaf, but it can be freely interpreted; other greens, seasonings, and combinations of meat can be used. Escarole or Swiss chard, for instance, can substitute for the spinach, and roasted peppers for the tomatoes.

Preheat the oven to 400°.

Place the bread in a small bowl and stir in the milk; set the mixture aside to let the bread absorb the milk.

*1 cup large soft white or whole-wheat
  bread crumbs*

¼ cup milk

1 small bunch spinach

1 pound ground beef

½ pound ground pork

¼ cup finely chopped onion

1 clove garlic, peeled and minced

8 cherry tomatoes

¼ cup (loose) Italian parsley leaves

1 egg

1 tablespoon Dijon mustard

Salt

Freshly ground black pepper

Wash the spinach, steam it just until it is wilted, refresh it under cold water, and drain it well.

Combine the meats in a bowl with the onion and garlic. With paper towels, pat away any excess moisture from the spinach. On a cutting board, chop the spinach, tomatoes, and parsley together; this also can be done in a food processor using the pulse button.

Stir the egg and the mustard into the bread mixture, then add this to the meat and stir to combine well. Add the chopped vegetables and a pinch of salt and pepper to taste and stir just to combine; do not overwork the mixture.

Shape the mixture into a loaf and place it in a baking pan or a cast-iron skillet. Put the pan into the oven and bake for about 40 minutes—test by cutting into the center to see if the meat has lost its raw color and that the juices are clear. Let the meatloaf rest for about 10 minutes before serving.

Macaroni Baked Under a Crust

4 servings

This is a slight modification of a recipe of my friend Nancy Nicholas, with whom I share an appetite for gossip traded over carbohydrates.

Salt

1 pound elbow macaroni or other
    small pasta

2 cups milk

1¼ cups veal or chicken broth

3 tablespoons butter

1 shallot, minced

2 tablespoons flour

Freshly ground white pepper

¾ cup coarse stale bread crumbs

2 ounces Gruyère or Swiss cheese,
    grated

½ teaspoon fresh thyme leaves or
    ¼ teaspoon dried

The components of this dish can be made ahead and combined before baking. After draining the macaroni well, place it in a bowl, stir in about a teaspoon of vegetable oil, and cover loosely with a kitchen towel.

Bring a large pot of water to a boil. Add a pinch of salt and drop in the macaroni. Cook just until barely tender—not quite al dente. Drain the pasta, refresh it under cold water, and drain again well.

Meanwhile, bring the milk and 1 cup of the broth just to a simmer and keep warm. Melt 2 tablespoons of the butter in a medium-size saucepan over moderate heat; when the butter ceases foaming, add the shallot and sauté for a minute. Stir in the flour and continue to cook for 2 minutes. Remove the pan from the heat and whisk in the milk and broth. When the mixture is smooth, return the saucepan to the heat and cook, stirring from time to time, until the sauce is thickened; season to taste with salt and pepper. Set the sauce aside to cool slightly.

Preheat the oven to 375°.

In a small bowl, combine the bread crumbs, cheese, thyme, and pepper to taste.

Lightly butter a gratin or other large, shallow baking dish. If your pan is large enough, pour the macaroni into the sauce and stir to combine well; if the pan cannot accommodate the pasta, do this in a large mixing bowl and pour the macaroni into the baking dish. Cover the surface of the macaroni with the bread crumb mixture; dot all over with the remaining butter. Place the pan in the oven. After about 10 minutes, drizzle about one third of the remaining broth over the surface, and, using a wooden spoon, press down gently on the crumbs. Do this two more times or until the broth is used up and the topping is crisp and golden brown. Let the dish rest for about 5 minutes before bringing it to the table.

PENNE WITH SWISS CHARD, ROASTED GARLIC, AND SPICY CRUMBS

4–6 servings

April 2000. Good

This is best with a substantial amount of Swiss chard; buy three bunches if they look small. If you prepare the garlic in advance, the dish can be completed in the time it takes to cook the pasta. If you have another way of roasting garlic, by all means use it for this.

I have one of those terra-cotta garlic roasters, which works quite well. Often, however, I forget about it until after I've wrapped the garlic in foil and tossed it into the oven.

Preheat the oven to 350°. Remove the outer, papery skin of the garlic. Place the garlic on a double thickness of heavy-duty aluminum foil, dribble a bit of the oil over it, and place it on the middle rack of the oven. Roast the garlic until it is tender when pierced with a cake tester or the tip of a very sharp knife, about 1 hour.

Cut the leafy part of the Swiss chard away from the tough stalks. Discard the stalks and cut the leaves into

1 head garlic

½ cup olive oil

2–3 bunches red or green Swiss chard

2–3 thick slices Swiss peasant or similar rustic-style white bread

Generous pinch crushed hot red pepper flakes (or to taste)

½ teaspoon fresh rosemary or ¼ teaspoon dried

¼ teaspoon dried thyme

¼ teaspoon dried oregano

Salt

1 pound penne or similar short pasta

½ cup chicken or vegetable broth, warmed

Grated Parmigiano Reggiano cheese

large slices. Wash the chard well in one or two changes of cold water and place in a colander to drain.

By hand, shred the bread into large crumbs (about ½ inch). Heat the remaining oil in a large heavy skillet over medium-high heat. Add the pepper and herbs to the warm oil and cook them for a few seconds, stirring all the while and taking care not to let them burn. Add the bread and continue to cook and stir until the crumbs are nicely golden brown. Remove the crumbs to a plate and sprinkle with salt. Return the pan to the heat.

Place a large pot of water over high heat. When it reaches a boil, put in a pinch of salt, drop in the pasta, and cook it until a bit under the al dente stage. Drain.

Place the Swiss chard into the pan that held the bread crumbs, cover, and steam until wilted, about 5 minutes. When the garlic is cool enough to handle, remove the cloves from their skins. Put the garlic in a small bowl, mash it with a fork, and pour in the broth; continue to mash until a rough puree is formed.

Turn the pasta into the pan with the Swiss chard. Add the garlic mixture and toss over medium heat to combine well and heat through; spoon into a serving dish, top with the crumbs, and serve at once. Pass the cheese at the table.

VARIATIONS:

½ pound finely shredded Savoy or green cabbage (about one quarter of a medium head) can be substituted for the Swiss chard.

3 hot or sweet Italian sausages, removed from their casings, crumbled and cooked, can be added to the final heating of the dish.

Spaghetti with Garlic Bread Crumbs

4 servings

Here, bread crumbs add texture and taste to pasta with olive oil and garlic, a modest elaboration of *spaghetti aglio e olio*—spaghetti with oil and garlic, the best dish to make when you think there's nothing in the house to cook.

2–3 large slices stale but not hard bread

½ cup olive oil

2–3 cloves garlic, peeled and minced

3–4 anchovy fillets in oil, drained

Salt

1 pound spaghetti or spaghettini

¼ cup chopped parsley leaves

Pepper

Crushed hot red pepper flakes (optional)

Put a large pot of water over high heat.

Place the bread in the bowl of a food processor and pulse until large crumbs form; you should have about 1½ cups.

Pour half the oil into a large skillet over medium heat. Add the garlic and sauté, just until the garlic begins to color—do not let it darken. Add the bread to the skillet and turn the heat up to medium-high. Stir constantly, until the bread has absorbed the oil and seems dry and toasted. Spoon the crumbs and garlic into a bowl.

Pour the remaining oil into a small pan over medium heat. Add the anchovies and cook, stirring from time to time, until the anchovies are more or less dissolved, about 3 minutes. Put the anchovy mixture into the bottom of the dish from which you will serve the pasta and keep the dish warm.

When the water comes to a boil, add a big pinch of salt and then the spaghetti. Cook just until al dente. Ladle a bit of the pasta cooking water over the anchovies in the serving dish, then quickly drain the pasta and turn it into the dish. Toss well, then toss again with the parsley and several grindings of pepper; sprinkle the bread crumbs over and serve at once. Pass the hot red pepper at the table.

GARLICKY ROAST PORK

6–8 servings

One 3–4-pound pork roast, boned, rolled, and tied

1 clove garlic, peeled and slivered

3 fresh sage leaves, minced

1½ tablespoons olive oil

1 head roasted garlic (page 82)

1 teaspoon coarsely ground mixed pepper (black, green, and white) or all black

1 teaspoon coriander seeds

Large pinch dried red pepper flakes, or to taste

1 teaspoon minced fresh rosemary leaves or ¼ teaspoon dried

¼ teaspoon salt

¼ cup dry coarse bread crumbs

Preheat the oven to 450°. Cut tiny slits into the flesh of the pork and insert the garlic slivers and about one third of the minced sage. Brush the roast with some of the oil, place it on a rack in a pan, and put it in the oven. After 15 minutes, turn the heat down to 425° and cook for about 45 minutes longer, just until the juices are clear.

Meanwhile, remove the roasted garlic from its cloves into the bowl of a food processor with the remaining sage, the pepper, coriander, red pepper, rosemary, and salt and pulse just to combine. Heat the remaining oil in a small skillet over moderately high heat. Add the bread crumbs and sauté them quickly, until they are just lightly colored. Add the crumbs to the garlic mixture, and combine them by pulsing two or three times.

Remove the roast from the oven. Coat the roast with the garlic mixture, patting it on with a spatula or, if the meat is not too hot, with your hand. Return the pork to the oven for 5 or 6 minutes, until it is nicely browned and crisped, but not burned. Let the roast rest for about 5 minutes before serving.

Rack of Lamb with an Herb Crust

2–4 servings

1 rack of lamb, oven ready (see Note)

1 tablespoon olive oil

1 tablespoon butter

1 shallot, minced

1 clove garlic, peeled and minced

½ cup fine fresh bread crumbs

1 tablespoon minced Italian parsley

1 teaspoon fresh thyme leaves or
   ¼ teaspoon dried

1 teaspoon minced fresh rosemary
   leaves or ¼ teaspoon dried

Salt

Freshly ground green or black pepper

1 tablespoon Dijon mustard

Preheat the oven to 450°. Place the lamb on a rack in a roasting pan and roast for about 25 minutes for medium-rare meat.

Meanwhile, place the oil and butter in a small skillet over moderate heat. Add the shallot and garlic and sauté for about 5 minutes, until they are soft but not browned. Add the crumbs to the pan and continue to sauté until the crumbs are very lightly browned. Off the heat, add the herbs, a pinch of salt, and several grindings of pepper.

Remove the lamb and lower the heat to 400°. Brush the surface of the rack with the mustard, then coat it with the bread mixture, gently pressing it on with your hands. Return the roast to the oven for 3–4 minutes to brown and crisp the crust, taking care not to burn the crumbs. Let the roast rest for 5 minutes before carving.

NOTE: Lamb racks tend to be quite small, around 3½ pounds, which will yield two substantial or three modest servings. If you can find one, a 4–4½-pound rack will serve four; otherwise, buy two quite small racks and plan on a bit left over. For six to eight servings, buy two racks and double the quantity of ingredients for the crust.

WHOLE STUFFED FISH

4 servings

One 3½–4-pound whole red snapper,
striped bass, or other fish, boned
and butterflied

1 cup small cubes from semolina,
white, or light whole-wheat bread

1 tablespoon olive oil plus additional
for the fish and the pan

½ small red onion, chopped

1 or 2 inner stalks fennel bulb,
trimmed, cleaned, and chopped

1 clove garlic, peeled and minced

½ cup small red or yellow tomatoes

2–3 strands saffron

1 handful of feathery tops from the
fennel bulb, chopped

¼ teaspoon fennel seeds

Salt

Freshly ground pepper

Hot red pepper flakes

Preheat the oven to 425°.

Wash and dry the fish thoroughly. Spread the bread on a baking sheet and place it in the oven to dry and toast the bread lightly, about 10 minutes; toss the cubes once or twice.

Pour the tablespoon of oil into a medium-size skillet over moderate heat. Add the onion, fennel, and garlic and cook, stirring, for about 5 minutes until they soften but do not brown. Add the tomatoes and saffron and cook for about 5 minutes longer, stirring—the tomatoes should begin to soften but not break down. Off the heat, stir in the fennel tops and seeds and salt, pepper, and hot pepper to taste. Finally, fold in the bread cubes.

Lightly brush the cavity of the fish with oil. Fill the cavity with the bread mixture—it will be quite full. Lightly coat with oil a roasting pan just large enough to hold the fish; place the fish in it; brush the top of the fish with oil and, if there is additional stuffing, add it to the pan. Place the fish in the oven and bake for about 20 minutes; the flesh should be flaky and no longer opaque. If the fish or the stuffing seems to be drying out before it is cooked through, tent the pan with aluminum foil.

CRAB CAKES

4 servings

This is the way I usually make crab cakes, with no more bread than is necessary and the best fresh lump crabmeat. Second-rate or canned crabmeat simply does not make for satisfactory crab cakes.

⅓ cup day-old coarse crumbs from any non-sourdough white bread, including French bread

Milk

1 egg

1 tablespoon mayonnaise

1 teaspoon Dijon mustard

2 tablespoons chopped Italian parsley

Salt

Freshly ground pepper

1 pound lump crabmeat, carefully picked over

1 tablespoon butter

1 tablespoon neutral-flavored cooking oil, such as safflower or canola

1 lemon, cut into wedges

Put the crumbs into a mixing bowl and add just enough milk to cover; let the bread sit for about 10 minutes. Squeeze out any excess milk, mix in the egg, then the mayonnaise, mustard, parsley, and a pinch of salt and pepper to taste. Add the crabmeat and mix everything together, just enough to combine; do not overwork the mixture. Shape the mixture into four or eight chubby patties—they may seem loose, but will hold together when cooked. If possible, place the crab cakes on a plate and chill for an hour or two before cooking.

Put the butter and oil in a large heavy skillet over moderately high heat. When the butter ceases foaming, add the crab cakes and cook until nicely browned on both sides, about 10 minutes. As the crab cakes cook, use a spatula to push in any errant lumps. Serve the cakes at once with the lemon.

Cooked salmon or codfish, flaked, can be substituted for the crabmeat.

A tablespoon of minced jalapeño pepper and/or a dash or two of red or green hot pepper sauce or a pinch of ground chile pepper can be added; cilantro leaves may be substituted for the parsley. These crab cakes are good served with salsa or guacamole or both.

For a crunchy coating, dredge the cakes in very finely ground dry bread crumbs or biscuit crumbs before cooking.

Vegetables
and
Side Dishes

Yesterday's bread can be incorporated into vegetable dishes as toppings for gratins or stuffings and even added to sautéed greens. The collection here also includes a tart made in a crust fabricated from day-old biscuits. Clearly, these are merely examples of what can be done and should inspire endless variations based on whatever is at hand.

BRAISED ONION GRATIN

CAULIFLOWER GRATIN

GRATINÉED ENDIVE

ARTICHOKE AND GREENS GRATIN

STUFFED VEGETABLES

NANA'S STUFFED ARTICHOKES

HARICOTS VERTS WITH ALMOND CRUMBS

SAUTÉED GREENS WITH BREAD CRUMBS

MUSHROOMS UNDER A CHEESE CRUST

ONION TART IN A BISCUIT CRUST

BRAISED ONION GRATIN

4 servings

This is a good side dish for a vegetable or egg entree, or to precede pasta or a main-course soup. The components can be prepared in advance and put together just before the final broiling. Pancetta or prosciutto can be substituted for the sausage, or, for a meatless version, grated Parmigiano Reggiano or pecorino cheese can be used.

1 tablespoon butter

1 tablespoon oil

1½ pounds small onions, peeled (see Note)

2 sprigs thyme

1 bay leaf

2 sprigs Italian parsley plus 10 leaves

Salt

Freshly ground pepper

½ cup chicken, beef, or vegetable broth

1 sweet Italian sausage (about ¼ pound)

⅓ cup coarse stale crumbs from white, whole-wheat, or semolina bread

Place the butter and oil in a medium-size skillet over medium-high heat. When the butter ceases foaming, add the onions. Cook the onions, turning them frequently, until they are as evenly browned as possible; do not let them get too dark or they will be bitter.

Add one sprig thyme, the bay leaf, the parsley sprigs, and pinches of salt and pepper to the pan; pour in the broth and bring it to a simmer. Lower the heat to maintain a simmer, cover the pan, and cook until the onions are tender but not soft when pierced with the tip of a sharp knife, 30–45 minutes.

With a slotted spoon, remove the onions to a gratin or shallow baking dish. Discard the herbs and pour off and reserve any remaining braising liquid.

Meanwhile, remove the sausage from its casing and break it up. Place a small skillet over medium heat; put the sausage into the pan and cook, stirring, until it has lost its raw color. Remove the pan from the heat and let the sausage cool a bit.

Place the bread crumbs, the leaves from the remaining sprig of thyme and the parsley leaves in the bowl of a food processor. Pulse a few times. Add the sausage and a grinding or two of pepper to the bowl and pulse four or five times to combine the mixture well and achieve a uniformly crumbly texture. This also can be accomplished by chopping on a cutting board.

Preheat the broiler. Distribute the sausage mixture over the onions and drizzle a bit of the reserved braising liquid over.

Place the gratin about 6 inches under the source of heat just until browned.

VARIATIONS:

The topping can be used as a stuffing for mushrooms, peppers, or onions.

NOTE: If you can find them, small flat onions are perfect for this; otherwise, any small onion or shallot is fine. Or use sliced regular onions.

CAULIFLOWER GRATIN

6 servings

1 large head cauliflower

Salt

1 tablespoon plus 1 teaspoon butter

1 large shallot, minced

1 cup heavy cream

1 tablespoon Dijon mustard
(optional)

1 teaspoon fresh thyme leaves

Freshly ground white or black pepper

½ cup grated Gruyère cheese

4 tablespoons fine dry bread crumbs

Preheat the broiler.

Trim away the leaves and core of the cauliflower and cut the larger florets into three or four pieces. With a paring knife, remove any brown spots on the florets; and wash the florets. Bring a large pot of water to a boil, add a large pinch of salt and the cauliflower; boil the cauliflower until tender but not mushy, 8–10 minutes. Pour the cauliflower into a colander, refresh it under cold water, and drain it well.

Place the tablespoon of butter in a saucepan over moderate heat. When the butter ceases foaming, add the shallot and sauté, stirring, until soft but not brown, about 3 minutes. Pour the cream and mustard into the saucepan, bring to a simmer, and cook without boiling until slightly thickened and reduced, about 8 minutes. Add the thyme, a generous amount of pepper, and half the cheese; season to taste with salt.

Pour the cream mixture and the cauliflower into a mixing bowl, and stir carefully to coat the vegetable. Pour the mixture into a buttered shallow gratin dish or baking pan approximately 9 by 12 inches. Combine the remaining cheese and the bread crumbs and sprinkle them over the cauliflower; dot the remaining butter over and place under the broiler until the topping is golden brown and crisped.

GRATINÉED ENDIVE

8 heads Belgian endive

Salt

Olive oil

Stuffing for Nana's Stuffed Artichokes (page 100)

Preheat the broiler.

Bring a large pot of water to a boil. Meanwhile, trim any bruised or broken leaves from the endive, and trim the stem end. When the water is boiling, add a pinch of salt and drop in the endive. Lower the heat and gently boil the endive 5–8 minutes; the endive should just seem tender when pierced with the tip of a sharp knife. Remove the endive from the water with tongs or a slotted spoon, refresh under cold water in a colander, and drain.

When they are cool, cut the endive in half from top to bottom and place them on paper towels, cut side down, to drain of excess moisture. Brush a baking dish large enough to hold the endive in one layer with oil. Lay the endive in the dish, brush them lightly, and sprinkle with the stuffing, pushing it a bit into spaces between the leaves.

Place the dish under the broiler, about 4–6 inches below the heat, for just a few minutes, to crisp the filling and lightly brown the endive. Serve hot or at warm room temperature.

ARTICHOKE AND GREENS GRATIN

6–8 servings

Serve this rich gratin with simply roasted or grilled lamb or chicken, or on its own for lunch or brunch. Other greens, such as arugula, as well as various herbs can be used, as long as the basic volume of ingredients is maintained.

Preheat the oven to 350°.

Remove the tough and broken outer leaves and any discolored tips from the escarole. Cut the escarole crosswise into 1-inch shreds; wash the shreds in a large amount of cold water, then drain them in a colander. Place a large skillet over medium heat and add the escarole; cover and steam just until wilted. Return the escarole to the colander, refresh it under cold water, and drain it well. Trim the spinach, wash it well, and steam, refresh, and drain in the same way.

Fill a large bowl with cold water. Cut the lemon in half and remove the seeds; squeeze the juice into the water and drop in the rind.

Trim the artichokes well at the stem end. Peel away all the dark outer leaves, until the inner pale leaves are exposed. Trim the artichokes across their tops, leaving only about 1½ inches attached to the bottoms. Cut the artichokes in half, then in quarters. Using the sharp tip of a paring knife, clean away the hairy choke at the centers. Cut the pieces into very thin slices. As you work, place the slices into the bowl of water. Drain the artichoke slices well, using paper towels to remove as much excess water as possible.

1 head escarole (about 1 pound)

2 bunches spinach (about 2 pounds)

1 lemon

2 globe artichokes

3 tablespoons olive oil

1 tablespoon butter

1 clove garlic, peeled and minced

2 shallots, minced

Salt

Freshly ground pepper

¼ cup chicken broth

3 eggs

1 cup grated Parmigiano Reggiano cheese

1 cup ricotta cheese

4 scallions, trimmed, cleaned, and thinly sliced, including 1 inch of the green tops

1½ cups coarse bread crumbs, from light whole-wheat bread if possible

Leaves from 2 sprigs rosemary, finely minced

Place 1 tablespoon of the oil and the butter in a large skillet over medium heat; when the butter ceases foaming, add the garlic and shallots and cook, stirring, for a minute or two. Add the artichokes to the skillet and cook, turning, for about 3 minutes; season with a pinch of salt and pepper to taste, add the broth, cover, and cook for 3 minutes longer. They should be tender but not soft. Remove the cover and set the artichokes aside to cool.

Place the drained escarole and spinach on a cutting board, and, with a large knife, chop them coarsely. Whisk the eggs in a mixing bowl, then stir in half the Parmigiano Reggiano and the ricotta. Add the artichokes, the chopped greens, and the scallions and combine well.

Place the bread crumbs, the remaining Parmigiano Reggiano, a few grindings of pepper, and the remaining olive oil in a small bowl; stir with a fork to combine well.

Butter a 10-inch square baking dish and turn the artichoke mixture into it, smoothing the top. Distribute the crumb mixture over evenly, cover the dish loosely with foil, place the dish in the oven, and bake for 15 minutes. Remove the foil, raise the heat to 400°, and bake for 10–15 minutes longer, until the top is browned and the mixture is bubbling.

STUFFED VEGETABLES

1 cup coarse crumbs from French, country,
 Swiss peasant, or whole-wheat bread

¼ cup chopped Italian parsley

¼ cup grated Parmigiano Reggiano cheese

1 clove garlic, peeled

2 tablespoons olive oil

Salt

Freshly ground pepper

The following is a good, very basic formula for hollowed-out tomatoes, onions, zucchini boats, peppers, or mushroom caps. It is enough for four tomatoes, onions, peppers, or zucchini boats or 10–12 large mushroom caps.

BASIC PREPARATIONS

TOMATOES

Cut in half horizontally, and squeeze gently to remove the seeds. The tomato can be filled in the cavities left behind, or, the flesh between them can be carefully removed with a paring knife or grapefruit spoon—don't cut through the wall—to create an entirely hollowed-out tomato. The removed flesh can be chopped and added to your stuffing.

VARIATION:

Replace the parsley, cheese, garlic, and olive oil with ½ cup Pesto (page 24); if the mixture seems too moist, increase the bread by tablespoons until it just holds together.

ONIONS

Plunge whole onions into a big pot of boiling water; when the water returns to the boil, cook the onions for exactly 1 minute. Remove and refresh immediately in a bowl of water and ice or in a colander under cold running water. When the onions are cool enough to handle, peel and trim them and use a melon baller to hollow out the centers, creating a cavity 1½ to 2 inches across.

PEPPERS

Cut in half from top to bottom; remove the seeds and membranes.

ZUCCHINI

Cut in half lengthwise, remove the seeds with a spoon, grapefruit spoon, or melon baller.

MUSHROOMS

Pull or cut out the stems; wipe the caps of any soil. The stems, trimmed and cleaned, can be chopped and added to the cooked ingredients for the stuffing.

VARIATIONS:

Most of the stuffing embellishments suggested for poultry (pages 71–73) can be used for vegetables.

NANA'S STUFFED ARTICHOKES

4 servings

This is how my grandmother—Nana Casini—made her artichokes. She was from Bari, in Apulia, but as she was just an infant when her parents emigrated, her cooking style was more or less generic Italian-American. She had a light touch, and she was particularly skilled with vegetables.

Artichokes were always a special treat for us, because they were fairly expensive compared to other produce. Nana once told me that, along with the more conspicuous reasons, her family despised organized gangsters because they had the power to control the market price of artichokes.

Trim the stem end of the artichokes so that they will be flat. Remove any tough, brown, or broken outer leaves and cut the tips off the others. Gently separate the leaves and wash the artichokes under cold water. Place them, upside down, in a colander to drain.

Cut the lemon into quarters and rub the tops and edges of the leaves of each artichoke with its own piece; reserve the lemon pieces.

4 globe artichokes

1 lemon

⅔ cup Italian parsley leaves

Pinch dried oregano

1 small clove garlic

1½ cups coarse crumbs from French baguette or other white bread

½ cup grated Parmigiano Reggiano or Romano cheese

Freshly ground black pepper

3 tablespoons olive oil

Chop the parsley and combine it with the remaining ingredients, reserving 1 table-spoon of oil. Divide the stuffing among the artichokes, pushing it gently between the leaves. Place the artichokes into a pot large enough to hold them comfortably and pour in water to a depth of about 2 inches.

Drizzle the remaining oil over the artichokes and place the lemon wedges, cut side down, on top.

Place the pot over medium-high heat. When the water begins to boil, lower the heat to keep it at a simmer, cover the pot, and let the artichokes steam until they are tender, 30–40 minutes. Test by tugging on a leaf—if it comes away easily, the artichokes are ready. Serve warm or at room temperature.

VARIATIONS:

This simple stuffing also can be used for mushrooms or tomatoes; or omit the cheese and sprinkle it lightly on clams on the half shell and broil them just long enough to crisp up the bread.

HARICOTS VERTS WITH ALMOND CRUMBS

4 servings

Place a medium pot of water over high heat; when the water comes to a boil, add the haricots verts and a large pinch of salt. Cook the beans for about 5 minutes, just until al dente. Immediately drain the beans in a colander and refresh under cold water. Drain the beans well.

1 pound haricots verts or young green beans, trimmed at the stem end and washed

Salt

2 teaspoons butter

1 shallot, minced

¼ cup roughly chopped almonds

½ cup toasted coarse bread crumbs

¼ cup chopped Italian parsley

Freshly ground pepper

Place the butter in a small skillet over moderate heat. When the butter ceases foaming, add the shallot and sauté for 2–3 minutes, until soft but not browned. Raise the heat to medium-high and add the almonds and bread crumbs; sauté, stirring, until the nuts and crumbs are toasted and crisp, but take care not to let them burn. Off the heat, add the parsley and salt and pepper to taste.

Toss the beans with bread mixture and serve.

VARIATION:

Substitute 1 clove garlic for the shallot, lightly toasted pignoli (pine nuts) for the almonds, and chopped basil or mint for the parsley.

Sautéed Greens with Bread Crumbs

4 servings

Finishing partially cooked greens with bread crumbs adds taste and texture. The method is simple.

2 pounds spinach, kale, or Swiss chard, tough leaves, stems, and ribs discarded, or 1 large head broccoli or cauliflower, florets and tender branches only, carefully washed

1 tablespoon olive oil

1 clove garlic, peeled and minced (optional)

½ cup coarse fresh crumbs from French or white or whole-wheat country-style bread

Salt

Freshly ground pepper

Steam the greens in a large skillet only in the water clinging to their leaves. As soon as the greens are wilted, refresh them under cold water in a colander and drain them well.

For broccoli or cauliflower, plunge the florets and branches into a large pot of boiling lightly salted water and cook for 3–4 minutes; they should remain slightly crunchy. Refresh under cold water and drain well.

Place the oil in a large heavy skillet over medium-high heat. Add the garlic and cook for a minute or so; add the crumbs and continue to cook just until everything is lightly browned; do not let the garlic or the crumbs take on too much color or they will become bitter. Add the vegetable and sauté, stirring, for 3 or 4 minutes, until the ingredients are combined and heated through. Season to taste with salt and pepper and serve.

Variations:

This dish is wide open to interpretations. Among other ingredients, onion, shallots, parsley, oregano, anchovies, Parmigiano Reggiano cheese, or hot red pepper flakes can be added to the sautéed crumbs; a dash of red wine vinegar at the end can brighten the flavors.

MUSHROOMS UNDER A CHEESE CRUST

8 servings

Serve this as the first course of a special dinner. By varying the types of mushrooms and the cheese used, it works well in almost any season, but it would be classic before grilled or roasted game birds or venison in the fall. I like the elegance of individual baking dishes or ramekins, which also make serving easier, but a shallow baking dish is fine.

Preheat the oven to 425°. Lightly butter eight four-ounce ramekins or a shallow ovenproof dish.

Wipe the mushrooms of dirt if necessary. Trim away the stems and slice the caps. Place the oil and butter in a large skillet over medium heat; when the butter ceases foaming, add the shallots and garlic and cook, stirring, until they are soft but not browned, about 2 minutes. Add the mushrooms, raise the heat to medium-high, and cook, stirring, until the mushrooms begin to give up their juices. Sprinkle the lemon juice over the mushrooms and continue stirring until most of the moisture in the pan has evaporated.

2 pounds cultivated, wild, or mixed fresh mushrooms

1 tablespoon olive or vegetable oil

1½ tablespoons unsalted butter

2 shallots, minced

1 clove garlic, peeled and minced

Juice of ½ lemon

1 tablespoon fresh thyme leaves

¼ cup fresh Italian parsley, chopped

3 tablespoons crème fraîche, sour cream, or heavy cream

Salt

Freshly ground white or black pepper

3–6 slices day-old French, white, or semolina bread

4 ounces fresh goat cheese

¼ cup veal or chicken stock

Remove the pan from the heat and stir in half the thyme, the parsley, the crème fraîche, and salt and pepper to taste. Spoon the mushrooms into the prepared ramekins.

Cut the bread into small dice, roughly ¼ inch square—you should have about 1¼ cups—and place them in a small bowl. Crumble the goat cheese into the bowl with the remaining thyme and white pepper to taste; toss to combine. Divide the bread mixture over the ramekins and gently press it down; the bread should be level with the tops of the ramekins. Drizzle the broth over and place the ramekins on a baking sheet. Put the sheet in the oven and bake for about 10 minutes, until the tops are crisp and brown and the cheese bubbly.

ONION TART IN A BISCUIT CRUST

8 servings

Like graham crackers, stale biscuits can make a delicious pie crust. This onion tart is just one example; any quiche or savory tart recipe can be adapted. With a green salad, this makes a fine lunch, brunch, or first course at dinner.

3 large stale biscuits

2 tablespoons butter, melted and cooled

Cayenne

Salt

Freshly ground black pepper

2 tablespoons olive oil

2 ounces pancetta, prosciutto, or bacon, finely chopped (optional)

1 clove garlic, peeled and minced

1½ pounds red, Vidalia, or all-purpose onions, thinly sliced (you should have about 2 cups)

3 eggs

1½ cups half-and-half

½ teaspoon fresh thyme or ¼ teaspoon dried

Freshly grated nutmeg

2 tablespoons grated Parmigiano Reggiano or Gruyère cheese

Break the biscuits into the bowl of a food processor. Add the butter, a pinch of cayenne, and salt and pepper to taste. Pulse until the ingredients begin to clump together.

Generously butter a 10-inch pie plate and turn the biscuit mixture into it. Using your fingers, press the mixture against the bottom and sides of the plate, bringing it just up to the rim; try to make a crust of even thickness. Cover the crust with plastic wrap; if you have one, set a 9-inch pie plate into it. In either case, put the plate into the refrigerator for 30 minutes or overnight.

Pour a few drops of the olive oil into a large skillet over medium heat. Add the pancetta and cook, stirring from time to time, until the pancetta is browned and has given up most of its fat. Add the garlic to the pan and sauté for a minute. Using a slotted spoon, remove the pancetta and garlic to a dish lined with paper towels. Pour off the fat in the pan.

Preheat the oven to 375°.

Pour the remaining oil into the pan and add the onions. Cook, stirring, until the onions are very soft but not browned; this will take 15–20 minutes.

Meanwhile, remove the second pie plate and the plastic wrap from the crust and place it in the oven on a rack set in the middle; bake for about 10 minutes, just until it takes on a medium golden brown color. Remove the crust from the oven and place it on a baking rack to cool. Lower the heat to 350°.

Whisk the eggs with the half-and-half, the thyme, several grindings of nutmeg, and salt and pepper to taste. Let the onions cool to room temperature, then combine them with the egg mixture. Distribute the pancetta and garlic over the bottom of the pie shell, then spoon the onion mixture in, smoothing the top. Sprinkle the cheese over and place the tart in the oven. Bake until the filling is set and the top is golden brown, about 30 minutes.

Let the tart rest for about 10 minutes before serving. Serve warm or at room temperature, cut into eight wedges.

SAVORY BREAD PUDDINGS

A good savory bread pudding is like a good casserole—in many menus, all that's needed in the way of accompaniments can be incorporated into one easy dish that can be made ahead. At the same time, a savory pudding is a fine main course for lunch or brunch or any light meal. The serving sizes given vary accordingly.

For tips on making bread puddings, see page 119.

CORN BREAD PUDDING WITH TOMATOES

DANIEL ORR'S POTATO AND WILD MUSHROOM BREAD PUDDING

ARUGULA-SCALLION BREAD PUDDING

ASPARAGUS PUDDING WITH RICOTTA

EGGPLANT AND RED PEPPER PUDDING

CORN BREAD PUDDING WITH TOMATOES

4–6 servings

In truth, there won't be enough corn bread left from the usual recipe—I have in mind the one on the back of the box that yields an 8-inch square—to execute this dish. But it is good enough to plan for ahead; double your favorite recipe and reserve half. This is a fine side dish for barbecued or grilled meats or chicken and a great addition to a buffet table. With a salad you can call it lunch.

Preheat the oven to 300°.

Cut the corn bread into strips about ½ inch wide by 2 inches long. If the bread is not dry to the touch, place it on a baking sheet and put it in the oven for 5–10 minutes, until it is dry but not browned.

Bring the broth to a low simmer and keep it warm over low heat. Melt the butter in a heavy saucepan. Add the scallions and sauté until they soften but do not take on color; add the jalapeño peppers and cook briefly. Stir in the flour and cook for about 2 minutes, stirring constantly.

Stale corn bread (see Headnote)

3 cups chicken broth

3 tablespoons unsalted butter

½ cup thinly sliced scallions, including 1 inch green tops (about 6 scallions)

1–2 minced jalapeño peppers

3 tablespoons flour

Salt

Freshly ground black pepper

3 cups cherry tomatoes, cut in half

½ cup cilantro leaves, roughly chopped, plus additional for garnish (optional)

½ cup shredded Monterey Jack cheese

Remove the pan from the heat and whisk in the broth. When the broth is fully incorporated and the mixture is smooth, place it over medium heat and cook, stirring frequently, until thickened, about 10 minutes. Remove the sauce from the heat and season to taste with salt and pepper.

Preheat the oven to 350°.

Lightly butter or oil a baking dish approximately 9 by 13 inches and line the bottom with the strips of corn bread. Distribute the tomatoes and the ½ cup cilantro over the bread. Carefully pour the sauce over and sprinkle on the cheese. Let the pudding sit for about 10 minutes to allow the bread to absorb the sauce, then place it in the oven. Bake the pudding for 30–45 minutes, until the top is golden brown and bubbly. The pudding will still be slightly saucy; let it rest for about 5 minutes, then serve, garnished with additional cilantro if desired, warm or at room temperature. If necessary, the pudding can be briefly reheated in the oven.

Daniel Orr's Potato and Wild Mushroom Bread Pudding

8 servings

Daniel Orr, the chef of New York's legendary three-star La Grenouille, is a young Midwesterner with impeccable French culinary training who has not yet reached his thirty-fifth birthday. This lovely dish only hints at his inventiveness. Daniel serves the pudding in individual molds with aged prime sirloin, but it is equally good with other roasts and game dishes.

Place 1 tablespoon of the olive oil into a medium-size skillet over medium heat. Add the onion and cook slowly until it is soft but not browned, about 10 minutes. Remove the cooked onion to a mixing bowl.

Trim the stems from the mushrooms, wipe away any soil, and slice the caps. Place the remaining oil and the butter in the skillet over medium heat, and, when the butter ceases foaming, add the garlic and mushrooms and cook, stirring, just until the mushrooms are softened and have given up their moisture. Place the mushrooms in the bowl with the onions. Add the potatoes, salt to taste, lemon zest, rosemary, thyme, sage, pepper mix, and Chinese spice powder.

Preheat the oven to 350˚.

2 tablespoons olive oil

1 small onion, sliced

1½ pounds mixed wild mushrooms, such as cremini, portobello, porcini, or shiitake

1 tablespoon butter

2 cloves garlic, peeled and minced

Salt

8–10 fingerling or other small potatoes (about 1¼ pounds), cooked and peeled

2 teaspoons coarsely grated lemon zest

2 teaspoons chopped rosemary

2 teaspoons chopped thyme

2 tablespoons sage, minced

½ teaspoon mixed pepper (white, black, Szechuan, and a pinch of crushed red pepper flakes ground together with a pinch of coriander seeds and a pinch of fennel seeds)

Pinch of ground Chinese 4- or 5-spice powder

5 eggs

2 cups heavy cream

1 cup milk

¼ cup grated Gruyère

¼ cup grated Parmigiano Reggiano cheese

3 cups large cubes dry stale bread (white, multi-grain, sourdough, or pumpernickel or a combination)

In a large bowl, whisk together the eggs, cream, and milk; combine the cheeses and add half to the egg mixture. Add the bread and mix well. Fold in the vegetables, combine well, and let the mixture rest for 20–30 minutes. Butter eight individual ovenproof ramekins or one large baking dish roughly 9 by 12 inches and spoon in the mixture. Sprinkle the remaining cheese over the tops. Place the dishes in a water bath and bake for 20–25 minutes or about 45 minutes for a large dish, until the custard is set and the top is lightly browned. If it seems to be browning too quickly, cover it loosely with foil.

VARIATION:

Blanched parsnips, carrots, celery root, or turnips can replace all or part of the potatoes.

ARUGULA-SCALLION BREAD PUDDING

6 servings

4 packed cups baby or young tender
   arugula or spinach

4 eggs

1 cup ricotta cheese

1 cup milk

1 cup chicken broth

Salt

Freshly ground white or black pepper

Cayenne

4 slices good white slicing bread or
   12 small slices French bread,
   diced (about ¼ inch)

2 tablespoons butter

4 large scallions or 8–12 small ones,
   trimmed and thinly sliced
   (about ¾ cup)

½ cup Italian parsley leaves, chopped

½ teaspoon fresh thyme leaves

Preheat the oven to 350°.

Wash the arugula well and drain it in a colander. If you are not using baby arugula, tear the leaves into pieces.

Break the eggs into a large mixing bowl, whisk them, then blend in the ricotta, milk, and chicken broth. Season the egg mixture generously with salt, pepper, and a pinch of cayenne. Stir the bread into the egg mixture.

Place the butter in a medium-size skillet over moderate heat. When the butter ceases foaming, add the scallions and cook, stirring, for about 5 minutes, until they are soft but not browned. Add the arugula, cover and steam for a minute or two, just until it is wilted.

Remove the arugula from the heat and let it cool for about 5 minutes. Stir the arugula, parsley, and thyme into the egg mixture.

Turn the mixture into a buttered baking dish about 8 by 11 inches or a 2-quart soufflé dish. Place the dish in a water bath, and bake for 35–45 minutes, until the custard is set and the top is golden brown.

Asparagus Pudding with Ricotta

4–6 servings

8–10 slices stale French baguette, sliced ½ inch thick

1 large bunch (about 1¼ pounds) asparagus

Salt

4 eggs

1 cup milk

1½ cups chicken or vegetable broth

Freshly ground white or black pepper

¼ cup thinly sliced chives

2 scallions, trimmed and thinly sliced

¼ pound prosciutto, finely chopped

1 cup ricotta cheese

Olive oil

Preheat the oven to 350°. If the bread is not quite dry, put the slices on a baking sheet and place it in the oven for 5 or 10 minutes.

Bring a medium pot of water to boil over medium-high heat. Snap the tough ends off the asparagus, then cut each stalk into three pieces 2 to 3 inches in length. When the water is boiling, add a pinch of salt and drop in the asparagus; when the water returns to the boil, cook the asparagus for 1 minute. Immediately drain the asparagus, refresh them under cold water, and drain again.

Whisk the eggs, then add the milk and broth; season generously with pepper. Stir the chives, scallions, and prosciutto into the egg mixture; add the ricotta, but do not mix it in thoroughly. Lightly oil or butter a baking dish approximately 9 by 12 inches and cover the bottom with the bread, overlapping the slices slightly.

If necessary, mop up any excess water from the asparagus with paper towels. Scatter the asparagus over the bread and carefully pour the egg mixture over. Let the pudding rest for about 5 minutes.

Place the pan in a water bath and bake for 30–40 minute, or until the custard is set but not dry when tested with a cake tester; serve warm or at room temperature.

Eggplant and Red Pepper Pudding

4–6 servings

Wash but do not peel the eggplant and cut it into slices about ⅓ inch thick. Lay the slices on paper towels and sprinkle on both sides with salt; cover with paper towels, pat gently, and set aside for about 15 minutes.

1 eggplant, about 2 pounds

Salt

2 large sweet red peppers, roasted, peeled, and seeded

2 cups chicken or vegetable broth

½ cup olive oil (approximate)

½ cup finely chopped onion

2 cloves garlic, peeled and minced

Hot red pepper flakes

1 generous teaspoon fresh oregano, chopped, or ¼ teaspoon dried

1 tablespoon flour

2 tablespoons tomato paste

10–12 slices stale French or Italian bread, cut into ½-inch slices

¼ cup chopped Italian parsley leaves

1 cup coarsely grated or roughly chopped Italian fontina cheese

2 tablespoons grated Parmigiano Reggiano or pecorino cheese

Preheat the broiler.

Cut the peppers lengthwise into ½-inch pieces and place them in a small bowl.

Pour the broth into a medium-size saucepan and bring it to a low simmer; keep the broth warm. Put 2 tablespoons of the oil in a medium-size saucepan over medium heat. Add the onion, garlic, hot pepper, and oregano and cook, stirring, for about 2 minutes. Add the flour and cook for 2 minutes longer, then stir in the tomato paste. Remove the pan from the heat and continue to stir until the mixture is smooth. Slowly pour in the broth while continuing to stir or whisk. Return the pan to medium heat and simmer until thick, stirring frequently. Set the sauce aside to cool slightly.

Pat the eggplant slices dry of any excess moisture and brush them lightly with olive oil. Lay the slices on a baking sheet or a sheet of heavy-duty foil and place them just a few inches below the heating element of the broiler. Broil the slices until they are lightly browned on both sides. Remove the eggplant and set it aside to cool slightly.

Lightly brush a 10-inch round or similarly proportioned baking dish with oil and line it with the bread. Lightly brush the bread with oil.

Preheat the oven to 375°.

Stir any juices that have accumulated around the peppers into the sauce, then stir in the parsley and the fontina. Alternating them casually, lay the eggplant and peppers over the bread. Slowly pour the sauce over and let the pudding sit for 10 minutes. Sprinkle the top with the grated Parmigiano Reggiano and place in the preheated oven. Bake for about 20 minutes, until the top of the pudding is lightly browned. Serve warm.

SWEET BREAD PUDDINGS

Few dishes yield as much pleasure as bread pudding. Comforting, tasty, and versatile, they also are very forgiving: seriously inept or scatter-brained is the cook who can fail to produce a decent, if not excellent, bread pudding.

Only two simple steps and a tip or two are needed to ensure a successful bread pudding. First, once assembled, give the bread some time—generally, 15 minutes or more—to absorb the custard or it will float to the surface rather than become assimilated with the other ingredients. Second, like all custards, bread pudding must be cooked in a water bath (or bain marie or bagno maria). This means that the dish the pudding is in is set into a larger pan like a roasting pan with hot water poured in to a level of about two-thirds its depth. The water bath creates a barrier between the pudding and the direct heat of the oven, which ensures a tender texture and prevents rubbery or brown edges.

Bread puddings cook slowly; a full-size one that yields 6–8 servings usually will need 50 or more minutes. Most of the puddings in the collection here are cooked in 350° ovens, but if your oven runs hot, you may want to cook them at 325°.

Bread puddings are better warm or at room temperature than hot, so they can and should be prepared ahead. A bread pudding that has been standing around for a few hours can be briefly reheated (a microwave oven is actually better for this than a conventional one) but they suffer from refrigeration.

PANETTONE BREAD PUDDING

———

CHOCOLATE BREAD PUDDING

———

ANOTHER CHOCOLATE BREAD PUDDING

———

JANE GARMEY'S ENGLISH SUMMER PUDDING

———

PEACH AND WHITE CHOCOLATE BREAD PUDDING

———

PUMPKIN-PUMPERNICKEL BREAD PUDDING

———

BREAD PUDDING WITH WINTER FRUITS

———

CRANBERRY PEAR BREAD PUDDING

PANETTONE BREAD PUDDING

Panettone has the virtue of keeping well for quite a long time. I have been fortunate to receive several gifts of this egg-rich Italian bread around Christmastime—more than can be consumed in a month of breakfasts. This dessert is the best way to dispose of the last of your panettone—even if it is still with you in February, as mine was when this recipe was developed. A rum-flavored crème anglaise or a bit of lightly whipped cream is a good accompaniment.

½ cup white raisins

¼ cup plus 1 tablespoon dark rum

½ cup orange juice

8–10 slices dry panettone, cut ½ inch thick

4 extra-large eggs

¾ cup sugar

1 cup heavy cream

3 cups milk

Grated zest of 1 orange

1 teaspoon vanilla

Place the raisins in a bowl and pour over ¼ cup rum and the orange juice. Set aside for 15 minutes.

Butter a baking dish approximately 9 by 12 inches. Place the panettone slices in the dish, overlapping them slightly and cutting them as necessary to cover the bottom.

Preheat the oven to 350°.

In a large bowl, whisk the eggs with the sugar until lightened, then whisk in the cream, milk, orange zest, vanilla, and remaining rum. Drain the raisins and distribute them over the panettone. Carefully pour the egg mixture over, pushing down gently on the bread if it begins to float. Cover the dish tightly with plastic wrap and let the pudding rest for about 10 minutes, again pressing down gently once or twice to be sure the bread is submerged and soaking up the custard.

Place the dish in a water bath and bake for about 1 hour, until set and lightly browned but not dry. Let the pudding rest for about 15 minutes before serving.

CHOCOLATE BREAD PUDDING

8 Servings

Very early one morning shortly after my family moved into our apartment, I awakened to the dreamiest fragrances imaginable. In fact, I thought I was still dreaming, or perhaps had fallen into Maurice Sendak's *Night Kitchen*. But no, butter and chocolate aromas *were* wafting through the bedroom windows, and the source was Ecce Panis, one of New York's excellent bakeries, which is just around the corner. A masterpiece there is the chocolate bread, and, since we tend to buy more bread than we can hope to consume, it often leads to this pudding. Crème anglaise flavored with a bit of whisky or brandy is an elegant alternative to the whipped cream.

The Ecce Panis loaf is a large round one; if you use one made in a conventional bread pan you may need eight slices.

6 large slices chocolate bread, about ½ inch thick (see Headnote)

6 egg yolks

½ cup sugar

2 cups heavy cream

1 cup milk

1 tablespoon vanilla

2 tablespoons confectioners' sugar (optional)

1 tablespoon unsweetened cocoa (optional)

Softly whipped cream (optional)

If necessary, put the bread on a baking sheet and place it in the oven to dry it thoroughly; do not let the bread toast. Lightly butter a baking dish approximately 9 by 12 inches and lay the bread in the bottom, overlapping the slices slightly; cut pieces of the bread as necessary to fill any gaps.

Preheat the oven to 350°.

Whisk the egg yolks, then whisk in the sugar and beat for a minute or so to lighten the mixture. Whisk in the cream, milk, and vanilla.

Slowly pour the custard over the bread and let it rest for about 15 minutes to allow the bread to absorb the custard. Put the baking dish in a water bath and place it in the oven. Bake for about 50 minutes, until the pudding is set but not dry. Combine the confectioners' sugar with the cocoa in a small sieve; dust the pudding with the mixture just before serving warm or at room temperature. Pass the whipped cream at the table.

VARIATIONS:

BLACK AND WHITE CHOCOLATE PUDDING: Roughly chop about ¼ pound good-quality white chocolate and distribute it over the bread before you pour the custard over; to prevent them from drying out, push the pieces of white chocolate into the bread if they seem to be too much on the surface. If you are serving the pudding with crème anglaise, add an additional ¼ pound chopped white chocolate to the finished sauce while it is still hot, and stir a few times as it melts.

"MOCHA" PUDDING: Substitute ½ cup strong black coffee (espresso is ideal) for an equal amount of the milk. Add 1 teaspoon very finely ground coffee to the confectioners' sugar and cocoa.

ANOTHER CHOCOLATE BREAD PUDDING

8 Servings

For this, you want stale but not dry or hard bread. Pulsing the bread in a food processor will achieve crumbs of the right size and texture.

½ pound semisweet chocolate

2 tablespoons butter

4 cups half-and-half

½ cup sugar

¼ cup unsweetened cocoa

⅛ teaspoon salt

4 eggs

1 teaspoon vanilla

¼ teaspoon almond extract

2 cups soft white bread crumbs

Preheat the oven to 325°.

Melt the chocolate and butter together in a double boiler or microwave oven. Heat the half-and-half in a large saucepan but do not let it boil, pour in the chocolate mixture, and combine them well.

Stir the sugar, cocoa, and salt together. In a large bowl, whisk the eggs, then beat in the sugar mixture; add the vanilla and almond extract. Slowly add the chocolate mixture to the eggs, whisking all the while. Stir in the bread crumbs.

Let the mixture rest for about 15 minutes, stirring a few times. Using a ladle, divide the mixture among eight 6-ounce custard cups or use one 2-quart ovenproof dish, such as a soufflé dish. Place the dishes in a water bath and put them into the oven. Bake individual dishes for about 30 minutes, a larger dish for about 45 minutes. The pudding is done when it is cooked through but still a bit wobbly on the surface—test with a sharp knife to be sure the interior is no longer liquid.

Jane Garmey's English Summer Pudding

6 servings

It would be foolish to attempt a better summer pudding than the one my friend Jane Garmey makes. It is a high moment when she carries her gorgeous purple-red creation to the table; I can't think of a better summer dessert. Jane's charming books, *Great British Cooking: A Well Kept Secret* and *Great New British Cooking*, changed what many of us thought of English food.

A good white bread with a tight crumb, a day old, is ideal for summer pudding.

3 pounds mixed fresh berries (any combination of raspberries, blueberries, cranberries, or red currants)

1 cup sugar (or more—up to 2 cups—if you are using a lot of cranberries or red currants)

8–10 slices day-old white bread, crusts removed

Whipped cream

Wash and rinse the fruit and remove any stems and leaves. Put the berries and the sugar into a medium saucepan over low heat. Stir frequently until the sugar has dissolved. Remove the pan from the heat.

Generously butter a 1-quart pudding bowl or similar deep dish. Line the bottom and sides with the bread, trimming it to fit into any gaps.

You should have 3–5 slices left.

(continued)

Carefully pour the berry mixture into the mold, smooth the top, and cover with the remaining bread, again cutting and fitting to fill any gaps.

Cover the bowl with a flat plate that fits neatly inside the rim and put on a heavy weight—an unopened can or two will do. Refrigerate the pudding overnight.

Before serving, remove the plate and run a knife gently around the inside of the bowl. Turn the pudding onto a serving dish. At the table, cut the pudding into wedges and serve it with generous dollops of cream.

PEACH AND WHITE CHOCOLATE BREAD PUDDING

6 servings

Peaches and white chocolate have an affinity that works especially well in this summer pudding. I don't share the disdain of some "foodies" for white chocolate, but I do think that the quality can be disappointing—too much sugar, waxy texture, and not enough cocoa butter taste. It is worth paying extra for a good brand like Caillebaut or Valrhona.

2 cups stale sturdy white or country-type bread, such as Swiss Peasant, cut into ½-inch cubes

2 large eggs

2 large egg yolks

½ cup sugar

1½ cups peach nectar or juice

2 cups half-and-half

1 teaspoon vanilla

4 medium barely ripe fresh peaches, well washed

12 ounces white chocolate

Place the bread in a large bowl. In another bowl, whisk the eggs and egg yolks with the sugar until lightened. Whisk in 1 cup of the nectar, half-and-half, and vanilla. Pour the egg mixture over the bread and stir to combine well; set aside for about 10 minutes, stirring from time to time.

Preheat the oven to 350°. Butter a dish approximately 9 by 12 inches.

Dry but do not peel the peaches. Cut the peaches from top to bottom into quarters, then in half horizontally. Roughly chop half the chocolate. Add the peaches and the chopped chocolate to the bread mixture and stir to combine. Spoon the mixture into the pan and set it into a water bath. Place the pudding into the oven and bake for about 45 minutes, until set but not dry.

Meanwhile, make a sauce. Place the remaining chocolate and nectar in the top of a double boiler and melt it slowly over barely simmering water. (This also can be accomplished in a microwave oven: Place the chocolate in a microwave-safe glass dish and cook on high for 30 seconds or more; take care not to scorch.) Whisk to combine as the chocolate melts. Set aside; if the sauce hardens, it can be softened by briefly—and slowly—reheating.

Serve the pudding warm or at room temperature, with a bit of sauce on the side.

Pumpkin-Pumpernickel Bread Pudding

8 servings

For the pastry phobic, this pudding delivers the familiar flavors and all of the satisfaction of pumpkin pie. Seedless rye bread or even white bread can be substituted for the pumpernickel. Your own pumpkin (or butternut squash) puree is best, but store-bought is acceptable—be sure to buy puree, not pumpkin pie filling.

2 cups stale pumpernickel cut into
  ½-inch cubes

2 eggs

⅓ cup white sugar

⅓ cup light brown sugar

2 cups pumpkin puree

1 cup milk

1 cup heavy cream

⅓ cup maple syrup

2 teaspoons cinnamon

½ teaspoon ground ginger

½ teaspoon ground nutmeg

⅛ teaspoon freshly ground white
  or black pepper

Whipped cream flavored with
  maple syrup

Preheat the oven to 350°. Butter a baking pan approximately 9 by 12 inches. Place the bread into a large bowl.

In another bowl, beat the eggs with the sugars until light and fluffy. Whisk or beat in the remaining ingredients, except for the whipped cream, until well combined. Pour the pumpkin mixture over the bread, stir, and let it rest for 15 minutes. Pour or spoon the mixture into the prepared pan and place in a water bath. Place the pudding in the oven and bake for 45 minutes or until set but not dry. Serve warm or at room temperature with the whipped cream.

BREAD PUDDING WITH WINTER FRUITS

8 servings

This is a particularly pleasing combination, but other dried fruits can be substituted for the apricots and pears, and dried cherries, cranberries, or blueberries can take the place of the raisins.

8–10 dried apricots

8–10 dried pears

½ cup white or dark raisins

1 orange, navel if possible

3 generous cups cubed stale challah, brioche, or other white bread (about 6 slices)

6 large eggs

¾ cup sugar

1 cup heavy cream

3 cups milk

¼ teaspoon freshly ground nutmeg

2–3 pieces of candied ginger, minced

¼ cup granola or steel-cut oatmeal

Confectioners' sugar

Preheat the oven to 350°. Butter a 9 by 12-inch rectangular baking pan or shallow oval casserole.

Roughly chop the apricots and pears; you should have ¾ of a cup of each. Place the chopped fruit in a bowl with the raisins. Grate the zest of the orange and reserve it. Squeeze the orange and pour the juice over the fruit.

Place the bread in a large bowl. Whisk the eggs, then beat them with the sugar. Mix in the cream, milk, nutmeg, ginger, and the orange zest. Pour the custard over the bread and let the mixture rest for 5 minutes. Drain the fruit, combine it with the bread, and pour everything into the pan. Sprinkle the granola over the top of the pudding, set the pan into a water bath, and place it in the oven.

Bake the pudding for 50 minutes to 1 hour, until it is set but not dry. Let it rest for 15 minutes before serving; serve warm or at room temperature, dusted with the confectioners' sugar.

CRANBERRY PEAR BREAD PUDDING

8 servings

Dark or white raisins or dried cherries can be substituted for the cranberries, and apple, pear, or orange juice can replace the eau-de-vie. Serve this as is or with vanilla ice cream.

½ cup dried cranberries

¼ cup pear eau-de-vie such as Poire William

3 medium ripe but firm Bosc or d'Anjou pears (about 1 pound)

2 tablespoons unsalted butter

1 cup sugar

6 large eggs

4 cups half-and-half

1 teaspoon vanilla

6 slices challah or brioche bread or 10 to 12 slices French baguette, about ½ inch thick

Confectioners' sugar (optional)

Place the cranberries in a small bowl and pour the eau-de-vie over.

Peel, core, and slice the pears into six pieces each. Melt the butter in a large skillet over medium heat and, when it ceases foaming, add ¼ cup sugar and the pears along with the eau-de-vie and cranberries. Cook, stirring gently, until the sugar melts and the mixture is warm. Carefully flame the mixture; shake the pan gently a few times, and set it aside once the flames die down.

Preheat the oven to 350°.

Whisk the eggs, then whisk in the remaining sugar, the half-and-half, and the vanilla. Lightly butter a baking dish and line it with the bread, overlapping the slices slightly. Distribute the pear mixture over the bread, then pour the custard over. Let the pudding rest for about 15 minutes, then set the dish in a water bath. Bake the pudding for about 45 minutes, until it is set but not dry. Serve warm or at room temperature, dusted with the confectioners' sugar.

FRENCH TOAST

Like French fries, French toast is not something many Americans think of as foreign food. It is among the favorite dishes—eggs and pancakes being the others—that make breakfast or brunch special. French toast is also thrifty and easy enough for a reasonably intelligent eight-year-old child to execute. Just about any bread will do, and the selection here takes advantage of several types, but to my mind challah and brioche produce the most elegant interpretations.

French toast requires no special skills or equipment but two important steps will ensure the very best results: Give your bread time to absorb the egg mixture, and turn it several times as it does so; and cook the soaked bread slowly, over moderate heat, so that it will cook through before becoming too brown—or burning—on the surface.

BASIC FRENCH TOAST

PANETTONE FRENCH TOAST with ORANGE SAUCE

FRENCH TOAST with BERRIES

RYE FRENCH TOAST with APPLES

WHOLE-WHEAT FRENCH TOAST with CARAMELIZED BANANAS

BISCUIT BREAKFAST SANDWICHES

BASIC FRENCH TOAST

2–4 servings

Just about any bread, including ones made with whole grains, can be used, but it is hard to beat challah or brioche bread for French toast. Panettone, another egg-rich bread, also is terrific. This is my basic recipe, quite open to flavor variations. Half-and-half can be used if you want a richer finish, the vanilla can be omitted, cinnamon or nutmeg can be added, and brown sugar can replace the white—or, sugar can be eliminated altogether. Butter and maple syrup are the American toppings of choice, but powdered confectioners' sugar and just about any fruit are equally tasty.

2 eggs

½ cup milk

Salt

Sugar

Vanilla

4 slices day-old (or older) bread, sliced ½ inch thick

1½ tablespoons butter

Beat together the eggs and milk, then add a pinch of salt, a pinch of sugar, and two or three drops of vanilla. Pour the mixture into a baking dish that will just hold the bread in one layer. Place the bread in the dish, then turn it. Leave the bread to soak up the mixture for 15 minutes or longer.

Heat a large heavy skillet over medium heat. Add the butter and when the foaming ceases, add the bread. Cook the bread, turning once, until it is golden brown on both sides. Lower the heat if it seems to be cooking too quickly or the egg mixture will not be cooked thoroughly. Serve at once.

Panettone French Toast with Orange Sauce

4 servings

This is also good with raisin bread. If you use cinnamon-raisin bread, omit the cloves or use very little.

3 eggs

1 cup half-and-half

4 large thick slices stale panettone; if the slices are very large, cut them in two

3 oranges

½ cup plus 1 tablespoon brown sugar

Ground cloves

Salt

5 tablespoons butter

¼ cup chopped almonds, pecans, or walnuts, or slivered almonds, toasted

Whisk the eggs and half-and-half in a baking dish large enough to hold the bread in one layer. Add the grated zest of 1 orange, the tablespoon of brown sugar, a pinch of cloves, and a pinch of salt. Place the bread into the egg mixture, turn it, and let it sit for 15 or more minutes or until the mixture has been absorbed, turning it over once or twice.

Meanwhile, place 3 tablespoons of the butter in a small skillet over moderate heat. When the butter is melted, add the remaining sugar and stir to incorporate. Squeeze the juice from the orange used for zest and stir it into the butter and sugar. Cook, stirring, until the sugar melts and the mixture is reduced, thickened, and syrupy—you should have ¾ cup of syrup.

Heat the remaining butter in a large heavy skillet over moderate heat. When the foaming subsides, add the bread and cook until the slices are evenly golden brown and cooked through.

Remove the skin and pith from the remaining oranges and cut them into segments, removing the membranes between them. Just before serving, place the segments in the warm sauce.

Divide the panettone among four serving plates and pour some syrup, along with orange segments, over. Top with the almonds and serve at once.

VARIATION:

The orange segments can be omitted.

NOTE: The panettone I used was rich with white raisins and currants. If yours is not, ¼ cup of either or ¼ cup of each can be plumped in the orange juice and then added to the custard.

French Toast with Berries

8 servings

This is the dish to serve for Mother's Day brunch or a similarly special, indulgent event. Any firm-textured white bread can be substituted.

Eight 1¼-inch-thick slices
    day-old challah or brioche

6 eggs

¼ cup plus 1 tablespoon sugar

Salt

2 cups half-and-half

1 teaspoon vanilla

2 cups mixed berries, such as
    strawberries, blueberries,
    and raspberries

2 or more tablespoons butter

½ pint crème fraîche (optional)

Mint leaves (optional)

If the bread still seems soft, place it on a cookie sheet in a 350° oven for 10 minutes, but do not let it toast.

Beat together the eggs, 1 tablespoon of sugar, and a pinch of salt, then add the half-and-half and vanilla. Place the bread in a pan or dish large enough to hold it in one layer. Pour the egg mixture over and let the bread stand until it has absorbed the mixture, about 15 minutes; using a metal spatula, carefully turn the bread once during this time.

Put the remaining sugar in a large skillet and place it over medium-high heat. Add the berries and stir carefully until the sugar dissolves and the berries are warmed through. Do this as quickly as you can so that the berries do not break down too much.

When the bread is ready, melt the butter in a large skillet over medium heat. When the butter stops foaming, add the bread and cook until golden brown on both sides. You probably will need to do this in two batches. Lower the heat if the bread seems to be browning too quickly or it will not cook through.

Place the cooked slices on each of eight individual plates and top with some of the berries, their sauce, about 1 tablespoon crème fraîche, and a mint leaf.

Rye French Toast with Apples

4 servings

4 large eggs

¼ cup sugar

1½ cups milk

½ teaspoon cinnamon

⅛ teaspoon ground nutmeg

Pinch ground ginger

Pinch salt

4 large thick slices stale rye bread or
8 slices from a narrow loaf

4 apples

4 tablespoons (or more) butter

½ cup sugar

½ cup maple syrup

½ cup chopped toasted pecans
(optional)

Whisk together the eggs and sugar, then whisk in the milk, cinnamon, nutmeg, ginger, and salt. Place the bread in a baking dish just large enough to hold the slices in one layer. Pour the egg mixture over and turn the slices. Set aside to allow the bread to soak up the custard, turning the slices once or twice

Peel and core the apples, then cut them into eight slices each. Heat 2 tablespoons of the butter in a large skillet over medium heat. Add the apples and sauté for about 1 minute. Turn the heat up to medium-high, add the sugar, and cook the apples until they are lightly caramelized; toss and turn them with a metal spatula. Remove the skillet from the heat and stir in the maple syrup.

Heat a large heavy skillet over medium heat and add the remaining butter. When the butter has ceased foaming, add the bread and cook until the slices are evenly browned on both sides. Remove the slices to a serving platter or individual plates and distribute the apple mixture and pecans over; serve at once.

WHOLE-WHEAT FRENCH TOAST
WITH CARAMELIZED BANANAS

3–6 servings

4 eggs

1 cup half-and-half

Coarsely grated zest of 1 orange

Freshly grated nutmeg

Salt

6 slices whole-wheat or multi-grain
bread, ½ inch thick

½ cup sugar

Juice of ½ orange

3 barely ripe bananas, cut into
large pieces

4 tablespoons butter

½ cup chopped toasted pecans
or walnuts

plain or vanilla-flavored yogurt

The inspiration for this comes from a dessert by Daniel Orr, the talented young chef of New York's renowned La Grenouille. Daniel makes his dish, a dessert, with baby bananas, which in fact are a variety of mature, small bananas from Ecuador; sometimes they are labeled "finger bananas." They are delicious and worth looking for. If you use them, serve two for each portion.

Whisk the eggs with the half-and-half, half the orange zest, several gratings of the nutmeg, and a pinch of salt. Pour the mixture into a baking dish that will just hold the bread in one layer. Add the slices, turn them, and set the dish aside to allow the bread to soak up the egg mixture.

Meanwhile, pour the sugar into a heavy skillet that will accommodate the bananas and place it over medium-high heat. Without stirring, melt the sugar and continue to heat it until it turns a rich caramel color; quickly and carefully whisk in the orange juice, then add the remaining zest. Lower the heat to medium and cook the mixture until it thickens slightly; add the bananas and continue to cook, until the bananas are heated and the sauce is syrupy. Remove the pan from the heat and stir in 2 tablespoons of the butter and a pinch of salt.

Heat the remaining butter in a large heavy skillet over medium heat. When the butter ceases foaming, add the bread and cook until the slices are golden brown on both sides. Place the slices on each of four plates and divide the bananas and their syrup among them. Top with the pecans and serve at once with some of the yogurt on the side.

Biscuit Breakfast Sandwiches

6 servings

By the time she was about three years old, my daughter Nina had discovered that the tips of strawberries and asparagus were the "best parts" and that day-old biscuits were "not so good." It does seem that biscuits never can be satisfactorily restored, but here they are so totally recycled their true essence is no longer an issue.

The fillings of these delicious little sandwiches can be varied; ham can replace the Canadian bacon, and other cheeses, or cheese alone, are just as good. The amount of chives may seem alarming, but I find that a critical mass of market-procured chives is needed to achieve the longed-for flavor. If you have chives in your garden or growing in a pot you can use fewer. Fresh sage would be good too.

Whisk together the eggs, buttermilk, a generous grinding of pepper, pinches of salt and cayenne, mustard, and chives. Pour the mixture into a baking dish just large enough to hold the biscuits.

2 eggs

1 cup buttermilk

Freshly ground black pepper

Salt

Cayenne

½ teaspoon dry mustard

1 bunch chives, snipped

6 large day-old biscuits

6 ounces sharp Cheddar, thinly sliced

6 thick (about ⅛-inch) slices
  Canadian bacon

2 tablespoons butter

Cut the biscuits in half; they may crumble a bit but this won't matter in the end. Poke each piece two or three times with a cake tester and spoon about a teaspoon of the egg mixture onto the cut side of each biscuit. Divide the cheese among the biscuit halves and place a slice of Canadian bacon on six, so that each sandwich will have bacon at the center. Carefully close the sandwiches, tucking in any wayward bits of biscuit and carefully place them in the dish.

After 15 minutes or so, using a spatula, turn the sandwiches and let them rest until the egg mixture is absorbed.

Place a large heavy skillet over medium heat and add the butter. When the foaming subsides, add the sandwiches, again pushing in any loose bits of biscuit. Cook the sandwiches until they are golden brown on both sides, turning them carefully. Lower the heat if they seem to be cooking too quickly so that they will be cooked through and the cheese will melt.

INDEX